U.S. Department of Transportation
Federal Transit Administration

Profiles of 511 Traveler Information Services Update 2009

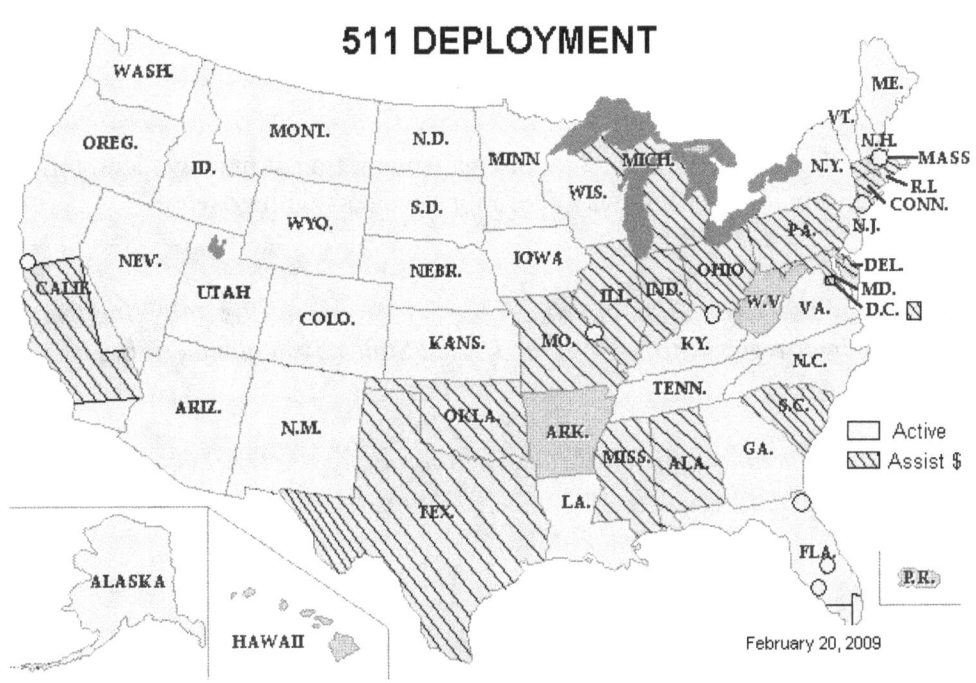

Nationwide Deployment Area

Report Number: FTA-TRI30-2009.1   *[http://www.fta.dot.gov/research]*

SEC. 5306. RESEARCH AND DEVELOPMENT; PUBLIC LAW 109-59

(a) In General. - The Secretary of Transportation shall carry out a comprehensive program of intelligent transportation system research, development, and operational tests of intelligent vehicles and intelligent infrastructure systems …

(b) Priority Areas. - Under the program, the Secretary shall give higher priority to funding projects that -
    (1) …
    (2) …
    (3) address traffic management, incident management, transit management, toll collection traveler information, or highway operations systems with goals of –

        (A) …
        (B) ensuring that a national, interoperable 5-1-1 system,… is fully Implemented for use by travelers throughout the United States by September 30, 2010; …

Source: Safe, Accountable, Flexible, Efficient Transportation Equity Act: A Legacy for Users (SAFETEA-LU). Online [http://www.fhwa.dot.gov/safetealu/legis.htm]

MAP KEY - COVER

Active indicates where 511 traveler information services are available.
Assist $ indicates locations that have received funding under the 511 Planning Assistance Program. Online at [*http://www.fhwa.dot.gov/trafficinfo/511.htm*]

U.S. Department of Transportation

Federal Transit Administration

Profiles of 511 Traveler Information Services Update 2009

Prepared by
Federal Transit Administration
Office of Research, Demonstration and Innovation
U.S. Department of Transportation
Washington, DC 20590

April 2009

Available From
Federal Transit Administration
Office of Research, Demonstration and Innovation
U.S. Department of Transportation
Washington, DC 20590

Available Online [http://www.fta.dot.gov/research]

Report Number: FTA-TRI30-2009.1

 *Traveler Information Service*

"511 will be a customer driven multi-modal traveler information service, available across the United States, accessed via telephones and other personal communications devices, realized through local deployed interoperable systems, enabling a safer, more reliable and efficient transportation system." - The National Vision for 511

Notice:

This document is disseminated under the sponsorship of the United States Department of Transportation in the interest of information exchange. The United States Government assumes no liability for its contents or use thereof.

The United States Government does not endorse manufacturers or products. Trade or manufacturer's names appear herein solely because they are essential to the objective of this report.

 **43 Telephone Services for Travelers**

FOREWORD

Profiles of 511 Traveler Information Services Update 2009 was prepared by the Federal Transit Administration's (FTA) Office of Research, Demonstration and Innovation to increase public awareness, access, and knowledge of the transit content within existing 511 traveler information services. This fourth edition provides descriptive profiles of each of the forty-three 511 traveler information services in operation within the United States, as of May 2009. It also includes a listing of the *Forty-Three 511 Systems: Areas of Commonality and Uniqueness*—highlighting areas of information these systems share and identifying those pieces of traveler information unique to specific systems. Information was obtained directly from each 511 call-in telephone number, which can be accessed by any traveler. 511 traveler information service is an easy way to obtain travel information anywhere in the country; it helps travelers make better decisions on travel routes and modes

Highlights *–January* 2009 usage statistics for 511 telephone services in North America reported to the 511 Deployment Coalition totaled 3,892,860 telephone calls. *Forty-five (45) 511 services* are available to the traveling public operating in 35 states and 2 Canadian provinces. 511 service was available to more than 150 million Americans (53%) and almost 1 million Canadians (3%). *Over 133 million calls nationwide* since its inception. *All 43 U.S. systems* have co-branded websites.

Twenty –four (24) systems provide public transit information [Arizona, Cincinnati/ Northern Kentucky, Central Florida, Georgia, Maine, Massachusetts, Minnesota, New Hampshire, New York, Northeast Florida, North Carolina, Rhode Island, Sacramento/Northern California, San Diego, San Francisco Bay Area, Southeast Florida, Southwest Florida, St. Louis Gateway, Tampa Bay, Utah, Vermont, Virginia, Washington State, Wisconsin]. More Online [http://www.fta.dot.gov/research]

The National 511 Traveler Information Service is under the guidance of the National 511 Deployment Coalition. The Coalition is comprised of the following major transportation organizations—American Association of State Highway and Transportation Officials, American Public Transportation Association, ITS America, and U.S. Department of Transportation. *Note*: 511 Resources are available at [http://www.deploy511.org]. See also [http://www.ops.fhwa.dot.gov/511/about511/history.htm]

Blank page

TABLE OF CONTENTS

FOREWORD iii
I. 511 DEPLOYMENT TABLE 1
II. 43 PROFILES 3

A. STATEWIDE TELEPHONE SERVICES 4
  Alaska 4
  Arizona* 5
  California Eastern Sierra 7
  Colorado 8
  Florida Statewide 9
  Georgia* 10
  Idaho 11
  Iowa 12
  Kansas 13
  Kentucky Statewide 14
  Louisiana 15
  Maine* 16

  Massachusetts* 18
  Minnesota* 20
  Montana 23
  Nebraska 24
  Nevada 25
  New Hampshire* 26
  New Jersey 27
  New Mexico 28
  New York* 29
  North Carolina* 32
  North Dakota 34
  Oregon 35

  Rhode Island* 32
  South Dakota 39
  Tennessee 40
  Utah* 41
  Vermont* 43
  Virginia* 44
  Washington State* 46
  Wisconsin* 48
  Wyoming 49

* 511 Systems with Transit Content

B. METROPOLITAN 511 SYSTEMS WITH TRANSIT CONTENT ...50
Cincinnati/Northern Kentucky ...50
Jacksonville/Northeast Florida ...52
Missouri – St. Louis Gateway ...53
Orlando/Central Florida ...54
Sacramento/Northern California ...56
San Diego ...59
San Francisco ...61
Southeast Florida ...64
Southwest Florida ...67
Tampa Bay ...68

III. FORTY-THREE 511 SYSTEMS: AREAS OF COMMONALITY AND UNIQUENESS ...69

DON'T LEAVE HOME BEFORE CALLING

I. 511 DEPLOYMENT TABLE
April 2009

DEPLOYMENT NAME	TRANSIT CONTENT	AUTOMATIC TRANSFER	WEBSITE	TELEPHONE
1. Alaska	No		http://511.alaska.gov	866-282-7577
2. Arizona	Yes	Yes,	www.az511.com	888-411-ROAD/7623
3. California Eastern Sierras	No		www.dot.ca.gov/dist9/	800-427-7623
4. Cincinnati/Northern Kentucky	Yes	Yes.	www.artimis.org.	513-333-3333
5. Colorado	No		www.cotrip.org	303-639-1111
6. Florida	No		www.fl511.con	866–511-3352
7. Georgia	Yes	Yes	www.511GA.org	877-MYGA511 (694-2511)
8.. Iowa	No		www.dot.state.ia.us/511	800-288-1047
9. Idaho	No		www.511.idaho.gov	888-432-7623
10. Kansas	No		www 511.ksdot.org	800-585-ROAD/7623 or 866-511-KDOT/5368
11. Kentucky Statewide	No		www.511.ky.gov	866-737-3767
12 Louisiana	No		www.511la.org	888-ROAD-511 (762-3511)
13. Maine	Yes + Ferry	Yes.	www.511maine.com	866-282-7578
14 Massachusetts	Yes	Yes	www.mass.gov/511]	617-374-1234
15. Minnesota	Yes	Yes.	www.511mn.com	800-542-0220
16 Montana	No		www.mdt.state.mt.ustravinfo511	800-226-7623
17 Nebraska	No		www.511nebraska.org	800-906-9069
18. Nevada	No		www.nevadadot.com	877-687-6237
19. New Hampshire	Yes, bus only	No.	www.nh.gov/dot/511	866-282-7579
20 New Jersey	No		www.njcommuter.com	866-511-NJDT--8 (6538).
21 New Mexico	No		www.nmroads.com	800-432-4269
22. New York	Yes	Yes	www.511ny.org	888-465-1169
23. North Carolina	Yes	Yes.	www.ncsmartlink.org/511	877-511-INNC/4662

DEPLOYMENT NAME	TRANSIT CONTENT	AUTOMATIC TRANSFER	WEBSITE	TELEPHONE
24 North Dakota	No		www.state.nd.us/dot/divisions/maintenance/511_nd.html	866-MY-ND-511 [866-696-3511]
25 Northeast Florida/Jacksonville	Yes	Yes	www.JAX511.com	866-511-3352
26. Oregon	No		www.TripCheck.com	800-977-ODOT/63 1-503-588-2941
27. Orlando [Central Florida]	Yes	Yes	www.fl511.com	866-510-1930
28 Rhode Island	Yes	No.	: www2.tmc.state.ri.us	888-401-4511
29. Sacramento/ Northern California	Yes	Yes	www.sacregion511.org	877-511-TRIP/874
30. San Diego	Yes	Yes	www.511sd.com	800-215-4551
31. San Francisco	Yes	No	www.511/org	510-817-1717
32. South Dakota	No		www.sddot.com/511.asp	866-MY-SD-511 [866-697-3511]
33. Southeast Florida	Yes	No.	www.southflorida511.com	866-914-3838
34. Southwest Florida	Yes	Yes	www.southwestflorida511.com	866-511-3352
35. St. Louis Gateway	Yes	Yes	www.traffic.com/St-Louis-Traffic/St-Louis-Traffic-Map.html	877-4STL-511 (478-5511)
36. Tampa Bay	Yes	No	www.511tampabay.com	800-576-3886
37. Tennessee	No		www.tn511.com	877-244-0065
38. Utah	Yes	No.	www.utah511.info	866-511-UTAH (8824)
39. Vermont	Yes	No	www.511vt.org	800-ICY-ROAD (429-7623)
40. Virginia	Yes	Yes	www.511virginia.org	800-578-4111
41. Washington State	Yes	Yes	www.wsdot.wa.gov/traffic/511	360-570-2301
42. Wisconsin	Yes	Yes	www.511wi.gov	866-511-9472
43. Wyoming	No		www.wyoroad.info	888-996-7623

II. 43 PROFILES

Active indicates where 511 traveler information services are available.
Assist $ indicates locations that have received funding under the 511 Planning Assistance Program.
Online at [http://www.fhwa.dot.gov/trafficinfo/511.htm]

Locations where 511 traveler information services are available:
- Alaska 511 • Arizona 511 • ARTIMIS - Northern Kentucky / Cincinnati
- Boston • Colorado 511 • Eastern Sierras, California • Florida Statewide 511
- Georgia 511 • Idaho 511 • Iowa 511 • Jacksonville 511 • Kansas 511
- Kentucky 511 • Louisiana • Maine 511 • Minnesota 511 • Montana 511
- Nebraska 511 • Nevada 511 • New Hampshire 511 • New Jersey 511 • New York
- North Carolina 511 • North Dakota 511 • Oregon 511 • Orlando / I-4, Florida
- Rhode Island 511 • Sacramento / Northern California Region 511
- San Diego 511 • South Dakota 511 • South Florida Smart SunGuide
- Southwest Florida 511 • St. Louis Gateway Guide 511 • Tampa Bay area 511
- TravInfo® - San Francisco Bay area • Tennessee 511 • Utah CommuterLink
- Vermont 511 • Virginia 511 Travel Information / I-81 • Washington State 511
- Wisconsin • Wyoming 511

Profiles of 511 Traveler Information Services   *Update April 2009*

A. STATEWIDE TELEPHONE SERVICES

Date: February 2009

Phone Number: 866-282-7577
Co-branded Website: http://511.alaska.gov

OPENING GREETING
"Welcome to Alaska 511 'Travel in the Know.' To request information on a specific highway press one '1' or say "highway." To request a local summary press two '2' or say "local." For the menu options press zero '0' or say "menu" at any time."
911 Citation? No

BASIC MENU
"**Menu**—here are all the categories: press one '1' or say "highway reports", press two '2' or say "local summaries", press three '3' or say "weather reports", press four '4' or say "ferries", press five '5' or say "comments on 511", press six '6' or say "Yukon road reports", press star '*' or say "help with 511". That's all the categories. To repeat this press the star '*' key or say "repeat"."
1. Highway Reports
2. Local Summaries
3. Weather Reports
4. Ferries
5. Comments on 511
6. Yukon Road Reports
* Help with 511

TRANSIT MENU
No

WEATHER INFORMATION
Yes—Alaska 511 Website provides four tabs; the last tab is *All Reports*. Click on this tab for tab labeled *Other Travel Info*. Click on this tab to access screen with Weather and Road Conditions; this provides access to the Road Weather Information System, (RWIS).

Connection/Referral to Transit Systems? No
Ability to navigate up the Menu? Yes

Transfer to other 511 systems? No
Transfer to what other systems? N.A.

Arizona 511

Date: February 2009

Phone Number: 888-411-ROAD (7623)
Co-branded Website: www.az511.com

OPENING GREETING
"Welcome to the Arizona 511 system. If you prefer to use our touch tone system press the star '*' key now, otherwise, you may make your selection by saying one of the following: roads, transit, airports, tourism or a quick report on the metro region." Which one would you like?"
911 Citation? No

BASIC MENU
1. Roads, press one '1'
2. Transit, press two '2'
3. Airports, press three '3'
4. Tourism, press 'four '4'
5. Quick Report [on the metro region], press five '5'
6. "To leave a comment at any time, press '8'"

TRANSIT MENU
1. **Phoenix Valley Metro**
   "Here is information provided by Phoenix Valley Metro Transit. If you'd like to be transferred to Valley Metro's customer service line, press the pound '#' key at any time during recording."

2. **Tucson Sun Tran System**
   "Here is information provided by Tucson Sun Tran Transit. If you'd like to be transferred to Sun Tran's customer service line, press the pound '#' key at any time during the recording."

3. **Native American Transits:**
   a. Hopi Tribe Transit System, press one '1'
   b. Navajo Transit System, press two '2'
   c. Salt River Pima America Transit Service, press three '3'

4. **Rural Areas - North**
   a. Bull Head Area Transit System. press one '1'
   b. Cottonwood Area Transit System, press two '2'
   c. Lake Havasu City Transit, press three '3'
   d. ShoLo Pinetop Four Seasons Transit, press four '4'
   e. Kingman Area Regional Transit, press five '5'
   f. Sidona Road Runner Transit System, press six '6'
   g. Helping Hands Agency Express, press seven '7'

Arizona 511  ... continued

5. **Rural Areas - South**
   a. City of Bisbee Transit System, press one '1'
   b. Coolidge Express, press two '2'
   c. Miami Transit, press three '3'
   d. Pima County Transit, press four '4'
   e. Sierra Vista's Vista Transit, press five '5'
   f. Sunsites Transportation in the City of Pierce, press six '6'
   g. Catholic Community Services, press seven '7'

WEATHER INFORMATION
No—Arizona 511 Website contains no weather information.

Connection/Referral to Transit Systems?
Yes, both summary information and option for direct connection to transit exists.
Ability to Navigate up the Menu?
Automatically transferred back to the Main Menu for no response.

Transfer to other 511 systems? No
Transfer to what other systems? N.A.

California Eastern Sierra

Date: February 2009

Phone Number: 800-427-7623
Co-branded Website: www.dot.ca.gov/dist9/

OPENING GREETING
"Welcome to the Caltrans highway information service. This highway information is the latest reported as of *current date and time*. At anytime during this call press the star '*' key to return to the main menu. Please say or enter the highway number."

911 Citation: No

BASIC MENU
[Only with highway number-- Note star '*' key did not work]

a. Southern California Area
b. Central California Area
c. Northern California Area

TRANSIT MENU
No

WEATHER INFORMATION
YES—California Eastern Sierra Website lists Weather as the fourth option under Local Information. Click on Weather to connect with the National Weather Service which provides notices of watches, warnings and advisories that are in effect for every county in California. This file is usually updated about every two minutes.

Connection/Referral to Transit Systems? No
Ability to Navigate up the Menu? No

Transfer to other 511 systems? No
Transfer to what other systems? N.A.

Colorado

Date: February 2009

Phone Number: 303-639-1111
Co-branded Website: www.cotrip.org

OPENING GREETING
"Welcome to the Colorado Department of Transportation 511 road information hotline. If this is an emergency, please hang up and dial 911. This information is also available on the web at: 'cotrip.org'. For travel conditions and road restrictions statewide, press one '1'; for scheduled construction or maintenance activities statewide, press two '2'; for transfer to surrounding States, press four '4.'

911 Citation? Yes

BASIC MENU
1. Travel Conditions and Road Restrictions Statewide
2. Scheduled Road Construction or Maintenance Activities Statewide
4. Transfer to Surrounding States

TRANSIT MENU
No

WEATHER INFORMATION
Yes - Colorado Website provides weather information: National Weather Service Links, Satellite, Air Pollution Advisory, Winter Weather, and more. You must provide the name/number of the highway/road before weather report is provided. The weather information is updated as new information becomes available.

Connection/Referral to Transit Systems? No
Ability to navigate up the Menu? N.A.

Transfer to other 511 systems? Yes, telephone numbers provided for each surrounding 511 system
Transfer to what other systems? Wyoming, Arizona, Kansas, Nebraska New Mexico, Oklahoma, Utah

Florida Statewide

Date: February 2009

Phone Number 866-511-3352
Co-branded Website www.fl511.com:

OPENING GREETING
"Welcome **to Florida's Statewide Sun Guide** travel information system. To switch to touch tone mode, press '88' or 'tt.' If you need instructions, say "help" or press the star '*' key. I can get you information on major highways throughout the State or more detailed information in Northeast Florida, Southeast Florida, Southwest Florida, Central Florida, or Tampa Bay. What would you like? Say "highways" or press one '1'; say "Northeast Florida" or press two '2'; say "Southeast Florida " or press three '3'; say "Southwest Florida" or press four '4'; say "Central Florida" or press five '5'; say "Tampa Bay" or press '6 '; or press the pound '#' key to tell us what you think. To get help, press the star key '*' or say "help.""

911 Citation? No

BASIC MENU
1. Highways
2. Northeast Florida
3. Southeast Florida
4. Southwest Florida
5. Central Florida
6. Tampa Bay
\# Tell us what you think
* Help

TRANSIT MENU
No

WEATHER INFORMATION
No—Florida Statewide 511 Website has no weather information

Connection/Referral to Transit Systems? No
Ability to navigate up the Menu? Yes

Transfer to other 511 systems? Yes
Transfer to what other systems? Northeast Florida, Southeast Florida, Southwest Florida, Central Florida, Tampa Bay

Georgia

Date: February 2009

Phone Number: 877-MYGA511 (694-2511)
Co-branded Website: [http://www.511GA.org]

OPENING GREETING
"Welcome to the Georgia Navigator 511 traveler information system, a service of the Georgia Department of Transportation. Please note you can always return to the previous question or menu at anytime by saying "know". To report an Incident, Accident, or Request Hero Motorist Assistance in Metro Atlanta press or say one "1"; for Highway Information press or say two "2"; for Transit or Ride Share Information press or say three "3"; for Airport Information press or say four "4"; for Tourism Information press or say five "5"; for Surrounding States press or say six "6"; to speak with a Traffic Operator at anytime press or say nine "9"."

911 Citation? No

BASIC MENU
1. Report Incidents, Accidents, Request Hero Motorist Assistance in Metro Atlanta
2. Highway Information
3. Transit or Ride Share Information
4. Airport Information
5. Tourism Information
6. Surrounding States
9. Speak with a Traffic Operator

TRANSIT MENU
For MARTA Information press or say one "1"; for Other Transit Information press or say two "2"; for Ride Share Information press or say three "3"; for AMTRAK Information press or say four "4"; for Greyhound Information press or say five "5"; to leave a Comment press or say seven "7"; to return to the Main Menu press or say star "*".

WEATHER INFORMATION
Yes—Georgia 511 Website provides up-to-date weather information for three major cities in the State: Atlanta, Macon, and Savannah. .

Connection/Referral to Transit Systems? Yes
Ability to navigate up the Menu? Yes

Transfer to other 511 systems? Yes
Transfer to what other systems? Florida, North Carolina, Tennessee

Idaho

Date: February 2009

Phone Number: 888-432-7623
Co-branded Website: www.511.idaho.gov

OPENING GREETING
"Welcome to Idaho Transportation Department's 511 travel information. You can also access traveler information on the internet at: 511.idaho.gov. You can interrupt this message at any time if you know the route number that you want. For help with this system press the pound key '#' or say "help"at any time. Main menu --for road reports press or say one '1'; for regional reports press or say two '2'; for truckers reports press or say three '3'; for tourism press or say four '4'; for other nearby States 511 press or say five '5'; to comment on the 511 system press or say six '6'.

911 Citation? No

BASIC MENU
1. Road Reports
2. Regional Reports
3. Truckers Reports
4. Tourism
5. Other Nearby States
6. Comments on the 511 System

TRANSIT MENU
No

WEATHER INFORMATION
Yes--Click on Idaho Website to access a Truckers Page. The next screen has seven tabs. Press the sixth tab for Weather. A map of the State is provided. Place the cursor on the area of the State for which information on the weather conditions are sought. A seven day forecast is provided.

Connection/Referral to Transit Systems? No
Ability to navigate up the Menu? Yes

Transfer to other 511 systems? Yes
Transfer to what other systems? Washington State, Oregon [Nevada, Utah, Wyoming, Montana, British Columbia—telephone numbers are provided for these States and a Canadian Province.]

Iowa

Date: March 2009

Phone Number: 800-288-1047
Co-branded Website: www.dot.state.ia.us/511

OPENING GREETING
"Welcome to 511 traffic information brought to you by the Iowa State Patrol and the Iowa Department of Transportation. Say the name of the city you want, or using your keypad enter the first three letters of the city followed by the pound '#' key. You could also say 'menu' to go to the main menu. **Menu** - here are all the categories you can choose from. When you hear the one you want just say it: highway traffic, road weather, statewide summary, regional summary, help with 511. That's all the categories. Just say the one you want."

911 Citation? No

BASIC MENU
1. Highway Traffic
2. Road Weather
3. Statewide Summary
3 Regional Summary
4 Help with 511

TRANSIT MENU
No

WEATHER INFORMATION
Yes—Iowa Website contains four tabs: the first tab is 511 information. Click this tab to get screen with five tabs, last tab is Weather. Click this tab to be connected to *Weatherview* and then click to the *Roadway Weather Information System* (RWIS).

Connection/Referral to Transit Systems? No
Ability to navigate up the Menu? Yes

Transfer to other 511 systems? No
Transfer to what other systems? N.A.

Kansas

Date: March 2009

Phone Number: 800-585-ROAD [7623] or 866-511-KDOT [5368]
Co-branded Website: [http://www.ksdot.org/offTransInfo/News05/easy_access.asp]

OPENING GREETING
"Welcome to the Kansas 511 traveler information system. If this is an emergency, hang up now and dial 911. At any time for assistance with menu options, say "help" for instructions. For additional information, visit our website at: 511.ksdot.org. For Kansas Turnpike system press or say one "1'; for Kansas highways press or say two '2'; for Motor Carrier information press or say four '4'; for information in other States press or say seven '7'.

911 Citation? Yes, in opening greeting

BASIC MENU
1. Kansas Turnpike System, press or say one '1'
2. Kansas Highways, press or say two '2'
4. Motor Carrier Information, press or say four '4'
7. Information in other States, press or say seven '7'
    a. For Nebraska Highways, press or say one '1'
    b. For Missouri Highways, press or say two '2'
    c. For Oklahoma Highways, press or say three '3'
    d. For Colorado Highways, press or say four '4'
    e. For Kansas Highways, press or say five '5'

TRANSIT MENU
No

WEATHER INFORMATION
Yes—Kansas Website provides two weather related tabs: Kansas Weather Conditions and Roadway Weather Stations. Current Kansas weather conditions updated every two hours. The Road and Runway Weather Information System (RWIS) provides a State map with up-to-date data on: Location, Surface Temperature (°F), Air Temperature (°F) and Air Humidity (%), Wind Speed (mi/h), Wind Gusts (mi/h), and Wind Direction.

Connection/Referral to Transit Systems? No
Ability to navigate up the Menu? No

Transfer to other 511 systems? Yes (contact numbers for Missouri, Oklahoma, Colorado)
Transfer to what other systems? Nebraska (must provide contact number) Missouri, Oklahoma, Colorado

Kentucky Statewide

Date: March 2009

Phone Number: 866-737-3767
Co-branded Website: www.511.ky.gov

OPENING GREETING
"Welcome to 511 traffic and travel information brought to you by the Kentucky Transportation Cabinet. You can also access traveler information on the internet at: www.511.ky.gov. You can interrupt this message at any time if you know the route number that you want. For help with this system press pound '##' or say "help" at any time. Main menu: for road reports press or say one '1'; for regional reports press or say two '2'; for nearby States 511 press or say three '3'; to request roadside assistance from State patrol press or say four '4'; for tourism information press or say five '5'; to comment on the 511 system press or say six '6'."
911 Citation? No

BASIC MENU
1. Road Reports
2. Regional Reports
3. Nearby States 511
    a. Ohio – Transfer
    b. West Virginia – Transfer
    c. Virginia—(866-695-1182)
    d. Tennessee—(877-244-0065)
    e. Missouri—Transfer
    f. Illinois—[800-452-IDOT(4368)]
4. Request Roadside Assistance from State Patrol
5. Tourism
6. Comment on 511 System

TRANSIT MENU - No

WEATHER INFORMATION
Yes—Kentucky Statewide Website provides four tabs; first tab is Weather. First tab contains two options: Kentucky Road Weather Info System (RWIS) or National Weather System. Short and long term predictions provided.

Connection/Referral to Transit Systems? No
Ability to navigate up the Menu? Yes

Transfer to other 511 systems? Yes
Transfer to what other systems? Ohio, West Virginia, Missouri

Louisiana 511

Date: March 2009

Phone Number: 888-ROAD-511 (762-3511)
Co-branded Website: www.511la.org

OPENING GREETING
"This is 511 travel information brought to you by the Louisiana Department of Transportation and Development. For a regional summary say "regional" or for a route based report say "route". You can also say "menu" to go to the main menu: [Note: Press zero '0'] Here are all the categories you can choose from. When you hear the one you want just say it; route reports, regional summary, weather, comments on 511and help with 511. That is all the categories. Just say the one you want. "

911 Citation: No

BASIC MENU
1. Route Reports, press one '1'
2. Regional Summary, press two '2'
3. Weather, press three '3'
4. Comment on 511, press four '4'
* Help with 511, press '*'

TRANSIT MENU
No

WEATHER INFORMATION
Louisiana 511 Website – You must provide the city name before weather report is provided for the day in that areas.

Connection/Referral to Transit Systems? No
Ability to Navigate up the Menu? Yes

Transfer to other 511 systems? No
Transfer to what other systems? N.A.

Maine

Date: March 2009

Phone Number: 866-282-7578
Co-branded Website: www.511maine.com

OPENING GREETING
"Welcome to 511 travel information brought to you by the Maine Department of Transportation. When you are done say "goodbye" and you can leave us your comments. Say the name of the city in the region you want or say 'menu' to go to the main menu. *[You can reach the main menu by pressing zero '0' at any time]* **Menu**—here are all the categories you can choose from. When you hear the one you want just say it: highway traffic, road weather, regional summary, Acadia National Park, tourism, ferry service and transit, other States, help with 511. That's all the categories. Just say the one you want."

911 Citation? No

BASIC MENU
1. Highway Traffic, press one '1'
2. Road Weather, press two '2'
3. Regional Summary, press three '3'
4. Acadia National Park, press four '4'
5. Tourism, press five '5'
6. Ferry Service and Transit, press six '6'
7. Other States, press eight '8'
* Help with 511, press star '*'

TRANSIT MENU
"For ferry service information in the State of Maine, say or press one '1'.
"For transit service information in the State of Maine, say or press two '2'."

1. **Ferry Service.** "For ferry service information in the State of Maine you can visit: [www.511maine.gov] and click on the link 'Explore Maine'. To hear more details on ferry services, you can choose from the following options; when you hear the one you want just say it: Maine State Ferry Services, Casco Bay Lines in Portland, Scotia Prince Cruises in Portland, and The Cat in Bar Harbor. That's all the options. Just say the one you want."

2. **Transit service.** "For bus information in the State of Maine you can visit [www.511maine.gov] and click on the link 'Explore Maine'. For Portland Transit information press '1'; for Lewiston-Auburn Transit information press '2'; for Bangor Transit information press '3'."

Maine  *... continued*

a. **Portland Transit Information**: "Call Metro at 207-774-0351 or I can transfer you. Would you like to be transferred? Say yes or no."

b. **Lewiston-Auburn Transit Information**. "Call CityLink at 207-777- 4563 or I can transfer you. Would you like to be transferred? Say yes or no."

c. **Bangor Transit Information**. "Call BACTS Community Connector at 207-947-0536 or I can transfer you. Would you like to be transferred? Say yes or no."

WEATHER INFORMATION
Yes—Maine Website provides seven tabs: *Weather Forecast* and *Weather Alerts*. Click on Weather Forecast to access twelve cities in Maine and two in New Hampshire for seven day weather forecast. Click on Weather Alerts which are issued and updated as needed.

Connection/Referral to Transit Systems? Yes
Ability to navigate up the Menu? Yes

Transfer to other 511 systems? Yes
Transfer to what other systems? Rhode Island, Vermont, New Hampshire

Massachusetts

Date: March 2009

Phone Number: 617-374-1234
Co-branded Website: http://www.mass.gov/511

OPENING GREETING
'This is Lieutenant Governor Tim Murray. Welcome to 511 Massachusetts sponsored by Mass Highway. If this call is an emergency, please hang up and call 911. Please enter a route number now followed by the star '*' key. If you want to report roadway defects, debris, or litter, press '321*'. If you would like to reach Highways for general or project related questions during business hours, press '322*.' To hear a complete list of the routes and services covered, please press zero '0'. To hear an up-to-the-minute report, please enter the route number you want followed by the star '*' key. After you hear a route report, you can request additional routes.'

911 Citation? Yes

BASIC MENU
'The following routes and services are available. You may interrupt this list at any point by entering the route number you desire.

1. For Boston and Cambridge roads including the Tip O'Neal Tunnel, Storrow and Memorial Drives and Soldiers Field Road, press 6*.
2. For Logan Airport, including the Callahan and Sumner Tunnels and Massport parking information, Press 5*
3. For the Mass Turnpike or Interstate 90, including Ted Williams Tunnel, press 90*.
4. For the Southeast Expressway, press 932*.
5. For MBTA Subway, bus, and commuter rail, and MBTA special event information, press T*.
6. For travel to and from Cape Cod and the Islands, press 7*.
7. To report litter or debris on or along the road, press 321* to contact Mass Highway.
8. To contact Mass Highway for general or administrative questions, press 322*
9. For information on car and Vanpools coordinated by MASS RIDES for Commuters, press 227*.
10. To transfer to the New Hampshire 511 information services, press 647* that's NH*
11. For all other routes, simply press the route number followed by the 'star' key.

Massachusetts  ... continued

TRANSIT MENU
1. For Commuter rail information, press T-1*
2. For Subways and Rapid Transit, press T-2*
3. For Bus and Water Transit Systems, press T-3*
4. For MBTA schedule and service changes, and for special event and holiday information, press T-4*.
5. To be connected to the MBTA Information System, press T-5*.

WEATHER INFORMATION
NO—Massachusetts Website does not currently provide weather information, however, detailed weather information including real time road and air temperatures will be provided once the Website is enhanced. Current 511coverage is limited to the Eastern part of the State.

Connection/Referral to Transit Systems? Yes, MBTA
Ability to Navigate up the Menu? Yes

Transfer to other 511 systems? Yes
Transfer to what other systems? New Hampshire

Minnesota

Date: March 2009

Phone Number: 800-542-0220
Co-branded Website: http://www.511mn.org/

OPENING GREETING
"This is 511 travel information brought to you by the Minnesota Department of Transportation. Say the name of the city in the region you want, or using your keypad enter the first three letters of the city followed by the pound '#' key. You can also say 'menu' to go to the main menu."

911 Citation? No

BASIC MENU
"Menu--here are all the categories you can choose from. When you hear the one you want, just say it."
1. Route Reports
2. Regional Reports
3. Transit
4. Weather
5. To Leave us a Comment on 511
* Help with 511, "You can press the star '*' key."

TRANSIT MENU
"Minnesota Transit—Say the name of the city in the region you want to hear information of nearby transit providers, or using your keypad enter the first three letters of the city followed by the pound '#' key."

1. St. Cloud
    a. St. Cloud MTC Metro Bus
    b. St. Cloud MTC Metro Bus Para-transit
2. Duluth
    a. Arrowhead Transit Dial-a-Ride and Route Deviation Service
    b. Duluth Transit Authority [DTA] Regular Route
    c. Duluth Transit Authority [DTA]—STRIDE [Special Transit Ride]
    d. Virginia Dial-a-Ride
3. International Falls
    a. Arrowhead Transit Dial-a-Ride and Route Deviation Service

Minnesota  ... continued

4. Minneapolis-St. Paul
    a. Laylaw (?) Transit Service operates a Dial-a-Ride Service
    b. Transit Team operates a Dial-a-Ride Service
    c. Metro Transit [MT]
    d. Minnesota Valley Transit Authority (MVTA)

5. Anoka
    a. Anoka County Traveler
    b. Metro Transit [MT]
    c. Northstar Commuter Coach

6. Detroit Lakes
    a. Becker County Transit
    b. Clay County Rural Transit [CCRT]

7. Bemidji
    a. Paul Bunyan Transit Dial-a-Ride and Route Deviation Service

8. Mankato
    a. Mankato Heartland Express
    b. Watonwan Take Me There Bus

9. Moorhead
    a. Clay County Rural Transit [CCRT]
    b. Moorhead Metro Area Transit [MAT]

10. Virginia
    a. Arrowhead Transit
    b. Virginia Dial-a-Ride

11. Annandale
    a. Annandale Heartland Transit. Dial-a-Ride and Route Deviation Service

12. Elk River
    a. RiverRider Public Transit Dial-a-Ride, Route Deviation and Subscription Service

13. Granite Falls
    a. Granite Falls Heartland Express Dial-a-Ride Service

14. St. James
    a. Watonwan Take Me There Bus Dial-a-Ride Service

Minnesota 511 ... continued

15. Arlington
    a. Trailblazer Transit

16. Stillwater
    a. Streets Circulator operates a Dial-a-Ride service
    b. Metro Transit
    c. Human Services operates a Dial-a-Ride service

17. Burnsville
    a. Metro Transit
    b. Dakota Area Resources and Transportation for Seniors Dial-a-Ride
    c. Minnesota Valley Transit Authority

18. Hibbing
    a. Arrowhead Transit
    b. Hibbing Area Transit
    c. Virginia Dial-a-Ride

19. Luverne
    a. Rock County Heartland Exp
20. Roseau
    a. Roseau County Area Transit Dial-a-Ride and Route Deviation
21. Crookston
    a. Tri-Valley Heartland Express Dial-a-Ride and Subscription Service
22. Olivia
    a. Renville Heartland Express Dial-a-Ride Service

WEATHER INFORMATION
Yes—Minnesota Website provides six tabs; the fourth tab is Weather. Click on *Traffic and Road Conditions* for current Weather Reports, Construction, Delays, Detours, and more. Information is available statewide, region or by major city.

Connection/Referral to Transit Systems? Yes
Ability to navigate up the Menu? Yes

Transfer to other 511 systems? No
Transfer to what other systems? N.A.

Montana

Date: March 2009

Phone Number: 800-226-7623
Co-branded Website: http://www.mdt.mt.gov/travinfo/511/

OPENING GREETING
"Welcome to the Montana 511 traveler information system. Also on the Web at www.mdt.mt.gov/travinfo/511/ . This system uses voice recognition. To enable, press the star '*' key now. For highway conditions, press one '1'; for Tourism Information, press five '5'; for information in other States, press seven '7'."

911 Citation? No

BASIC   ENUM
1. Highway Conditions
5. Tourism Information
7. Information in Other States
    a. For North Dakota Highways, press one '1'
    b. For South Dakota Highways, press two '2'
    c. For Wyoming Highways, press three '3'
    d. For Idaho Highways, press four '4'
    e. For Montana Highways, press five '5'
        1. For route specific information, press one '1'
        2. For regional summary information, press two '2'
        3. For past summary information, press '3'

TRANSIT MENU
No

WEATHER INFORMATION
Yes—Montana Website provides fourteen tabs; the last tab is Weather Information. There are four options; one is *Other Reports* which provides 6-10 day weather outlook or hourly weather roundup among other weather related choices.

Connection/Referral to Transit Systems? No
Ability to navigate up the Menu? No

Transfer to other 511 systems? Yes
Transfer to what other systems? Idaho (1-888-432-7623)

Nebraska

Date: March 2009

Phone Number: 800-906-9069
Co-branded Website: http://www.511nebraska.org/ndortip/index.jsp

OPENING GREETING
"Welcome to the Nebraska 511 Traveler Information System. If this is an emergency, hang up now and dial 911. This system uses voice recognition. To enable, press the star '*' key now." For highway conditions, press one '1'; for information in other States press seven '7.'

911 Citation? Yes, in opening greeting

BASIC MENU
1. Wyoming Highways, press one '1'
2. Kansas Highways, press two '2'
3. South Dakota Highways, press three '3'
4. Weather information in other neighboring States, press four '4'
    a. For Iowa Highways, please call 1-800-288-1047
    b. For Missouri Highways, please call 1-800-222-6400
    c. For Colorado Highways, please call 1-303-639-1111
5. Nebraska Highways, press five '5'.

TRANSIT MENU: No

WEATHER INFORMATION
YES—Nebraska Website provides eight tabs; the third tab is Weather. Click on Weather to access Current Weather for Nebraska Town/City or Interstate 80 for Two Days. *Direct Links to Regional Radar* for Nebraska & surrounding states Updated every 15-30 minutes

Connection/Referral to Transit Systems? No

Ability to navigate up the Menu? No

Transfer to other 511 systems? Yes
Transfer to what other systems? Iowa.

Nevada 511

Date: March 2009

Phone Number: 877–687–6237
Co-branded Website: www.nevadadot.com

OPENING GREETING
"Welcome to the Nevada 511 traveler information system. If this is an emergency, hang up now and dial 911. For highway conditions, press or say one '1'; for information in other States, press or say seven '7'. Command options include main menu. To return to the main menu say "back " to navigate backward to the menu. Repeat to hear the current main options again. At any time for assistance with menu options say "help" for instructions."

911 Citation? Yes

BASIC MENU
1. Highway Conditions
7. Highway Information in Other States

TRANSIT MENU: No

WEATHER INFORMATION
Yes -- Nevada Website [http://safetravelusa.com/nv/] provides five options; the last one is Winter Driving Safety. Click on this option to access a screen with six choices; the second is Nevada Weather Forecast. Click on locations on the State map for current site specific weather observations. This data includes: Hourly (State Weather Roundup), State Forecast, Zone Forecast, Short Term (NOWCASTS), Forecast Discussion, Weather Summary, Public Information, Climate Data, Hydrological Data, Watches, Special Weather Statements, Warnings and Advisories, Fire Weather, Current Observations

Connection/Referral to Transit Systems? No
Ability to navigate up the Menu? Yes

Transfer to other 511 systems? Yes
Transfer to what other systems?
- For California Highways, please call: 1-800-427-7623 (not a 511 connection)
- For Utah Highways, please call: 1-866-511-8824,
- For Arizona Highways, please call 1-888-411-7623 ,
- For Idaho Highways, please call 1-888-432 7623 ,
- For Oregon Highways, please call 1-800-977-6368.

New Hampshire

Date: March 2009

Phone Number: 866-282-7579
Co-branded Website: www.nh.gov/dot/511

OPENING GREETING
"Welcome to 511 travel information for New Hampshire. You can interrupt this message at any time if you know the route number that you want. For help with this system press pound-pound '##' or say "help" at any time. **Main Menu** --for road reports press or say one '1', for regional reports press or say two '2', for nearby States 511 press or say three '3', to comment on the 511 system press or say four '4', for help with the 511 system press pound -pound '##' or say "help"."

911 Citation? No

BASIC MENU
1. Road Reports
2. Regional Reports
3. Nearby States 511
4. Comment on 511 System
Help with 511 System

TRANSIT MENU: No

WEATHER INFORMATION
Yes—New Hampshire Website provides thirteen tabs; fourth one is *Weather Conditions*. This screen provides two weather related options: Current Weather Conditions and Extended Weather Forecasts. Click on a city on the State map provided to view the current statewide weather conditions in New Hampshire. Extended 7-day forecasts are provided for twelve cities.

Connection/Referral to Transit Systems? No
Ability to navigate up the Menu? Yes

Transfer to other 511 systems? Yes
Transfer to what other systems? Maine, Vermont, Massachusetts, Rhode Island, Quebec

New Jersey

Date: March 2009

Phone Number: 866.511.NJDT (6538).
Co-branded Website: http://www.nj511.info

OPENING GREETING
"Welcome to New Jersey's 511 travel information hotline. This information is also available on line at: www.nj511.info. I can get you information on traffic conditions or easy pass. Which one would you like? Say "what are my choices" for a list of everything you can do or say "help". Now what can I get you. Here is a list of everything you can do with the 511 system. If you hear the one you like feel free to interrupt me. You can ask for traffic conditions or easy pass. If you would like to give us your feedback press seven seven '77' at anytime. To hear these again say "repeat". Which would you like? "

911 Citation: No

BASIC MENU
1. Traffic Conditions
2. Easy Pass
77. Feedback

TRANSIT MENU: No

WEATHER INFORMATION
No—New Jersey Website does not provide weather information.

Connection/Referral to Transit Systems? No
Ability to Navigate up the Menu? Yes

Transfer to other 511 systems? No
Transfer to what other systems? N.A.

New Mexico

Date: March 2009

Phone Number: 800-432-4269
Co-branded Website: www.nmroads.com

OPENING GREETING
"Welcome to the New Mexico road advisory hot line. If this is an emergency, please hang up and dial 911. Road information is updated as conditions change. Road conditions were last updated on [changes periodically each day]. For Statewide road conditions press one '1', for traffic information on I-40 or I-25 in the Albuquerque area press two '2', for Statewide construction information press three '3', for road conditions in surrounding States press eight '8'. To rehear these options press the pound '#' key. To disconnect press the star '*' key."

911 Citation: Yes

BASIC MENU
1. Statewide Road Conditions
2. Traffic Information on I-40 or I-25 in the Albuquerque area
3. For Statewide Construction Information
8. For Road Information in Surrounding States
    1) Arizona press one '1' (transfered to 511)
    2) Colorado press two '2' (call 1-303-639-1111)
    3) Texas press three '3' (transfered to Texas road traveler information system)
    4) Oklahoma press four '4' (transfered to Oklahoma road traveler information system)

TRANSIT MENU: No

WEATHER INFORMATION
YES—New Mexico Website connects to [http://nmroads.com/] which provides Weather Advisories with links to the National Weather Service (NWS), New Mexico Weather, and New Mexico Radar. National Weather Service provides current conditions and a detailed seven-day forecast. *Note: To reach Weather information, please scroll down left side of webpage.*
Connection/Referral to Transit Systems? No.
Ability to Navigate up the Menu? Yes

Transfer to other 511 systems? Yes
Transfer to what other systems? Arizona.

New York

Date: April 2009

Phone Number: 888-465-1169
Co-branded Website: www.511ny.org "Get Connected To Go"

OPENING GREETING
"Welcome to 511 NewYork. I can transfer you to any of the following regions: the Adirondack region including the Westburg and Watertown metro areas, the Capital region including the Albany and Saratoga metro areas, the Central region including the Syracuse and Utica metro areas, Finger Lakes-Rochester, Hudson Valley-Catskills, Long Island region, the New York City metro region, Niagra-Buffalo, or the Southern Tier region including the Hornell, Elmira, Binghamton metro areas. "

911 Citation: No

BASIC MENU

1. Adirondack Region
    a. Traffic conditions
    b. Public transportation /ferries
    c. Para-transit
    d. Ride share
    e. More choices:
       1. Airports
       2. Quebec Canada traveler information system
       3. Switch to another New York 511 Region
       4. Feedback
2. Capital Region
    a. Traffic conditions
    b. Public transportation
    c. Para-transit
    d. Ride share
    e. More choices:
       1. Airports
       2. Switch to another New York 511 Region
       3. Feedback
3. Central Region
    a. Traffic conditions
    b. Public transportation
    c. Para-transit

New York 511 ...continued

  d. More choices:
   1. Airports
   2. Quebec Canada traveler information system
   2. Switch to another New York 511 Region
   3. Feedback
4. Finger Lakes/Rochester
  a. Traffic conditions
  b. Public transportation
  c. Paratransit
  d. Ride share
  e. More choices:
   1. Airports
   2. Switch to another New York 511 Region
   3. Feedback
5. Hudson Valley/Catskills
  a. Traffic conditions
  b. Public transportation/ferries
  c. Paratransit
  d. Ride share
  e. More choices:
   1. Airports
   2. New Jersey 511
   3. Switch to another New York 511 Region
   4. MTA Agency
   5. Feedback
6. Long Island Region
  a. Traffic conditions
  b. Public transportation/ferries
  c. Paratransit
  d. Ride share
  e. More choices:
   1. Airports
   2. New Jersey 511
   3. Switch to another New York 511 Region
   4. MTA Agency
   5. Feedback
7. New York City Metro Region
  a. Traffic conditions
  b. Public transportation/ferries
  c. Paratransit
  d. Ride share

New York  ...continued

      e. More choices:
         1. Airports
         2. New York City 311
         3. New Jersey 511
         4. Switch to another New York 511 Region
         5. MTA Agency
         6. Feedback
8. Niagara/Buffalo
    a. Traffic
    b. Public transportation
    c. Paratransit
    d. Other 511s
    e. More choices:
        1. Airports
        2. Switch to another New York 511 Region
        3. Feedback
9. Southern Tier Region
    a. Traffic
    b. Public transportation
    c. Paratransit
    d. More Choices
        1. Airports
        2. Switch to another New York 511 Region
        3. Feedback

TRANSIT MENU – Yes. (See "public transportation" under Basic Menu.)

WEATHER INFORMATION
No—New York Website does not connect to a specific weather tab. Under a *road conditions* tab, however, you can receive information on the Winter Travel Advisory system which describes driving conditions on many of New York State's most-traveled roads. Conditions are displayed on a zoomable, color-coded map based on snowplow drivers' reports. Conditions are updated at least every four hours during winter months and more frequently during storms..

Connection/Referral to Transit Systems? Yes.
Ability to Navigate up the Menu? Yes

Transfer to other 511 systems? Yes
Transfer to what other system? New Jersey

North Carolina

Date: March 2009

Phone Number: 877-511-INNC [4662]
Co-branded Website: www.ncsmartlink.org/511

OPENING GREETING
"Welcome to the North Carolina 511 travel information line brought to you by the North Carolina Department of Transportation. Say 'main menu' to return to this menu, or say 'help' for assistance. You can also press '88' or 'TT' for touch tone at any time. When you hear the option you want, just say it. Now would you like highways, public transportation, weather, other services or other States."

911 Citation? No

BASIC MENU
1. For traffic, press one '1'
2. For public transportation, press two '2'
3. For weather, press three '3'
4. For other agencies that serve travelers, press four '4';
5. To be connected to 511 systems in neighboring States, press five '5'; or
\# Press the pound key '#' to tell us what you think.
0. You can get Help by pressing zero '0'.
9. To return to this menu, press nine '9' at any time.

TRANSIT MENU
A. *BUSES.* Currently, information is available for the following areas. For Charlotte Area Transit, press one '1'; for Triad Area Transit, press two '2'; for Cabarrus County Transit, press three '3'; for Iredell County Transit, press four '4' or enter the city or county code for which you would like transit information. The code for Cities are CI or 24 and the first four letters of the city name followed by the star '*' key. The code for counties are CO or 26 and the first four letters of the county name followed by the star '*' key. You can find a complete list of the cities, counties, roads, and metro areas we cover on our website at [www.nc511.com].

1. **Charlotte Area Transit.** "The Charlotte Area Transit System uses a live agent Monday through Friday 6:00 a.m. to 6:30 p.m. At other times automated information is available. I can transfer you to CATS at: 866-799-CATS [2287], press one '1'. If you do not want to be transferred, press two '2'.
2. **Triad Area Transit.**
    a. For Hi-Tran in High Point.
       "I can transfer you to Hi-Tran at: 1-336-889-7433.
       Press one '1' if you want to be transferred; press two '2' if you don't."

North Carolina 511 ... continued

    b. For Guilford County Transportation.
       I can transfer you to Guilford County Transportation at: 336-641-4848.
       Press one '1' if you want to be transferred; press two '2' if you don't."

    c. For PART (Piedmont Authority for Regional Transportation).
       "I can transfer you to PART at: 336-883-PART [7278].
       Press one '1' if you want to be transferred; press two '2' if you don't."

    d. For Greensboro Transit Authority.
       "I can transfer you to Greensboro Transit Authority at: 336-335-6499.
       Press one '1' if you want to be transferred; press two '2' if you don't.

    e. For Winston-Salem Transit Authority.
       "I can transfer you to Winston-Salem Transit Authority at: 336-727-2000.
       Press one '1' if you want to be transferred. Press two '2' if you don't."

3. **Cabarrus County Transit.** "I can transfer you to the Cabarrus County Transportation System at: 704-920-7433. Press one '1' if you want to be transferred; press two '2' if you don't."

4. **Iredell County Transit.** "I can transfer you to the Iredell County Area Transportation System at: 704-873-9393. Press one '1' if you want to be transferred; press two '2' if you don't."

B. **RAIL.** "I can transfer you to: 800-BY-TRAIN [800-298-7246]. Press one '1' if you want to be transferred; press two '2' if you don't."

C. **FERRIES.** "I can transfer you to the North Carolina Department of Transportation, Ferry Division; your gateway to the Outer Banks at: 800-BY-FERRY [800-293-3779]. Press one '1' if you want to be transferred; press two '2' if you don't."

WEATHER INFORMATION
Yes—North Carolina Website provides eight tabs; the last one is Weather. This screen accesses weather data for five State regions. Weather information is updated daily at any time as weather conditions warrant. A seven day forecast is also provided.

Connection/Referral to Transit Systems? Yes
Ability to Navigate up the Menu? Yes

Transfer to other 511 systems? Yes
Transfer to what other systems? Virginia, Tennessee, Georgia

North Dakota

Date: March 2009

Phone Number: 866-MY-ND-511 [866-696-3511]
Co-branded Website: [http://www.dot.nd.gov/divisions/maintenance/511.htm]

OPENING GREETING
"Welcome to the North Dakota 511 Traveler Information System. If this is an emergency, hang up now and dial 911. Road conditions are updated daily 5:00am to 9:00pm central time including holidays. North Dakota DOT wishes to remind you "don't crowd the plow" This system uses voice recognition. To enable, press the star '*' key now. For North Dakota highways, press one'1'; for South Dakota highways, press two '2'; for Montana highways, press three '3'; for Minnesota highways, press four '4'.

911 Citation? Yes

BASIC MENU
1. North Dakota Highways
2. South Dakota Highways
3. Montana Highways
4. Minnesota Highways

TRANSIT MENU
No

WEATHER INFORMATION
Yes--Website provides Weather information. Click on Weather Forecast to access the next screen for: State & District Forecasts which provides the ability to view forecast information statewide or on a district-by-district basis. The next screen provides a State map. Place the cursor on the area of the State for the two day forecast for that area.

Connection/Referral to Transit Systems? No
Ability to Navigate up the Menu? No

Transfer to other 511 systems? No
Transfer to what other systems? N.A.

Oregon

Date: March 2009

Phone Number: 800-977-ODOT [6368] or the toll number is: 503-588-2941
Co-branded Website: www.TripCheck.com

OPENING GREETING
"Welcome to the Oregon Department of Transportation's TripCheck traveler information system.
Main Menu—this menu has seven options: for road conditions by highways press one '1' or say "highway"; for road conditions in mountain passes press two '2' or say " mountain pass"; for road conditions in major cities press three '3' or say "major cities"; for commercial vehicle restrictions press four '4' or say "restriction"; for information about Oregon chain requirements press five '5' or say "chain"; to hear traveler information phone numbers for bordering states press six '6' or say "other States"; for information about ODOT's [Oregon Department of Transportation] improved road condition reporting system press seven '7' or say "information". To repeat these options at any time, you may press zero '0' or say "main menu".

If you have questions about how to use the system or you would like to provide *feedback* please call 1-888-ASK-ODOT during regular business hours, that's 1-888-275-6368 and choose option four '4.' This report may not contain all state road conditions, construction and/or maintenance work in Oregon. Motorist can expect traffic restrictions, lane closures, detours and short delays. Watch for signs, flaggers and pilot cars and please bundle up and drive safely. You can find more detailed information on the internet at: TripCheck.com."

911 Citation? No

BASIC MENU

1. Road Conditions by Highway
2. Road Conditions in Mountain Passes
3. Road Conditions in Major Cities
4. Commercial Vehicle Restrictions
5. Oregon Chain Requirements
6. Traveler Information Phone Numbers for Bordering States
7. Information about ODOT's Improved Road Condition Reporting System
0. Repeat above options.

TRANSIT MENU – No

Oregon  ...continued

WEATHER INFORMATION
Oregon—Website contains weather information provided via a State map which is subsectioned into nine areas. Place cursor on an area to view a seven day forecast.

Connection/Referral to Transit Systems? No
Ability to Navigate up the Menu? Yes

Transfer to other 511 systems? Yes (telephone numbers provided)
Transfer to what other systems? Washington—800-695-7623, Idaho—888-695-7623, Nevada—not a 511 connection, California—800-427-7623

Rhode Island

Date: March 2009

Phone Number: 888-401-4511
Co-branded Website: www2.tmc.state.ri.us

OPENING GREETING
"Welcome to 511 travel information brought to you by the Rhode Island Department of Transportation. If this is an emergency, please hang up and dial 911. Your feedback will help to improve this system. To end this call say 'goodbye' and you can leave us your comments. Say the name of the city or town you want, or hold on for Rhode Island statewide reports."

911 Citation: Yes

BASIC MENU - *[Note: You must press zero '0' to get to the main menu.]*

"Menu. Here are all the categories you can choose from. When you hear the one you want just say it: highway traffic, road weather, statewide summary, regional summary, transit, tourism, other States, help with 511. That's all the categories. Just say the one you want."
1. Highway Traffic
2. Road Weather
3. Statewide Summary
4. Regional Summary
5. Transit
6. Tourism
7. Comment on 511
8. Other States

TRANSIT MENU
1. For Bus Service Information in the State of Rhode Island press or say one '1'
    a. RIPTA [Rhode Island Public Transit Authority] "Call 401-781-9400 or 1-800-244-0444 or visit on the web at: www.ripta.com"
    b. Bonanza Bus Lines: "Call 401-751-8800 or 1-800-556-3815 or visit on the web at: www.bonanzabus.com"
    c. Greyhound Lines: "Call 401-454-0790 or 1-800-231-2222 or visit on the web at :www.greyhound.com"
2. For Train Service Information in the State of Rhode Island press or say two '2'
    a. Amtrak: "Call 1-800-872-7245 or visit on the web at: www.amtrak.com"
    b. Providence Train Station: "At 401-727-7379"
    c. Massachusetts Bay Transportation Authority: "At 1-800-392-6100 or visit on the web at www.mpta.com"

Rhode Island 511 ... continued

3. For Ferry Service Information in the State of Rhode Island press or say three '3'
   a. Bristol Improvements and Hog Island press or say one '1' or "Call 401-253- 9808".
   b. Interstate Navigation Company to Block Island press or say two '2' or "Call 401-783-4613 or 1-860-442-7891 or 1-860-442-9553 or visit on the web at: www.blockislandferry.com "
   c. Island Hi-Speed Ferry to Block Island press or say three '3' or Call 1-877-733-9425 or visit on the web at: www.islandhispeedferry.com"
   d. Jamestown and Newport Ferry Company press or say four '4' or Call 401-423-9900 or visit on the web at: www.jamestownri.com"
   e. Montauk Long Island, New York to Block Island press or say five '5' or "Call 516-668-5709 or 1-800-MON-TAUK [666-8285] or visit on the web at: www.vikingfleet.com"
   f. RIPTA Providence to Newport Ferry Service press or say six '6' or Call 401-781-9400 or visit on the web at: www.ripta.com"
   g. Vineyard Fast Ferry press or say '7' or "Call 401-295-4040 or visit on the web at: www.vineyardfastferry.com

4. For Airport Information in the State of Rhode Island press or say four '4'
   TF Green Airport: "Call 401-737-8222 or 1-888-268-7222 or visit on the web at: "www.pvdairport.com"

WEATHER INFORMATION
Yes—Rhode Island Website [http://www2.tmc.state.ri.us] contains traffic management center which has seven options of which five and six are two weather-related choices: Weather Forecast and Weather Alerts. A map of the State is provided and you click on Providence or Newport for current and seven day forecasts.

Connection/Referral to Transit Systems? Yes
Ability to navigate up the Menu? Yes

Transfer to other 511 systems? Yes
Transfer to what other systems? Maine, Vermont and New Hampshire, (Massachusetts--1-617-374-1234--not a 511 system)

South Dakota

Date: March 2009

Phone Number: 866-MY SD 511 [866-697-3511]
Co-branded Website: www.sddot.com/511.asp

OPENING GREETING
"Welcome to the South Dakota 511 traveler information system. If this is an emergency, hang up now and dial 911. For South Dakota highways press one '1'; for North Dakota highways press two '2'; for Nebraska highways press three '3'; for Montana highways press four '4'; for Wyoming highways press five '5', Minnesota highways press six '6'; for weather information in other neighboring States press seven '7'."

911 Citation: Yes

BASIC MENU
1. South Dakota
2. North Dakota
3. Nebraska
4. Montana
5. Wyoming
6. Minnesota
7. Weather information in other neighboring States;
    - For Iowa highways, please call: 1-800-288-1047 (511 number)

TRANSIT MENU
No

WEATHER INFORMATION
Yes—South Dakota Website contains a Traveler Information box with ten tabs; the second *Safe Travel USA*. Click on this tab to access a national map. Move cursor to South Dakota. Click on any major city site and receive daily weather information.

Connection/Referral to Transit Systems? No
Ability to Navigate up the Menu? No

Transfer to other 511 systems? No
Transfer to what other systems? N.A.

Tennessee

Date: March 2009

Phone Number: 877-244-0065
Co-branded Website: www.tn511.com

OPENING GREETING
"Welcome to 511 travel information brought to you by the Tennessee Department of Transportation. Menu: to hear up-to-date traffic information say "traffic conditions" or press one '1', for weather conditions say "weather" or press two '2', to transfer to a 511 system in a neighboring State say "other States" or press three '3', to leave a comment with your feedback on the system say "comment" or press four '4', for assistance on using the system say "help" or press five '5'. To hear these options again say "repeat" or press star '*'. Please make your selection."

911 Citation: No

BASIC MENU
1. Traffic Conditions, press one '1'
2. Weather, press two '2'
3. Other States, press three '3'
4. Comment, press four '4'
5. Help, press '5'
* Repeat

TRANSIT MENU
No

WEATHER INFORMATION
See *Basic Menu* above. Weather information is provided for the day as it affects highways or cities. You must provide the highway number or name of the city.

Connection/Referral to Transit Systems? No
Ability to Navigate up the Menu? Yes

Transfer to other 511 systems? Yes
Transfer to what other systems? North Carolina, Kentucky, Virginia, Georgia

Utah

Date: March 2009

Phone Number: 866-511-UTAH (8824)
Co-branded Website: www.utah511.info

OPENING GREETING
"Welcome to Utah's 511 travel information service. Main Menu—here are all your choices. When you hear the one you want just say it: traffic, public transit, road conditions, ferries, or surrounding States. You can also say "help" or press zero '0' at any time."
911 Citation: No

BASIC MENU
1. Traffic
2. Public Transit
3. Road Conditions
4. Ferries [Lake Powell]
5. Surrounding States

TRANSIT MENU
1. **Buses**. "Say 'stop' to cancel. Local buses generally run from 6:00 am to midnight on weekdays and 7:00 am to midnight on Saturdays. Buses have more limited hours on Sundays. For more information say "connect me" or visit 'rideuta.com'. You can pay your fare on the bus and get a free transfer to another bus or TRAX, or buy your fare at a vending machines at any TRAX station. A day pass can be purchased for same day use at vending machines at TRAX stations. Check 'rideuta.com' for more UTA bus information."

2. **TRAX Light Rail.** "Say 'stop' to cancel. TRAX Light Rail runs from 5:30 am to 11:00 pm Monday through Saturday. Late night service runs on Friday and Saturday nights. The last train leaves downtown at 1:00 am; for updates visit 'rideuta.com'. During special events TRAX adds later and more frequent evening service. During peak commute hours TRAX stops at stations every 10 minutes, during off peak times it stops every 15 to 3 0 minutes. Free transfers are allowed between TRAX and local buses with a valid ticket or transfer. A day pass can be purchased for same day use at vending machines at TRAX stations."

3. **Flex Tran.** "Say 'stop' to cancel. Flex Tran, also known as paratransit service, offers curb to curb shared ride service for eligible riders from 5:00am to 11:00 pm Monday through Saturday. Limited service is available on Sunday and limited late night service is available Friday and Saturday. This service must be reserved at least one day in advance and operate in same area and during the same hours as the fixed route service. For more information on paratransit services, contact Flex Tran directly at: 801-287-7433."

Utah 511 ...continued

4. **Ride Share.** "Say 'stop' to cancel. UTA's Ride Share program offers an alternative to driving alone including carpool and vanpool matches with other commuters who live and work in the same area who want to share a ride. Other Ride Share services include: alternate work hours, bicycling commuting, van leasing and eco-pass (a discounted transit pass sponsored by your employer). Visit 'utarideshare.com' for more information.'

WEATHER INFORMATION

Website provides three tabs. The third tab is Weather Forecast. Click this tab to access a screen which will provide daily weather projections for each city in the State.

Connection/Referral to Transit Systems? Yes
Ability to Navigate up the Menu? Yes

Transfer to other 511 systems? Yes
Transfer to what other systems? Arizona, Nevada, Idaho, Wyoming, Colorado, New Mexico.

Vermont

Date: March 2009

Phone Number: 800-ICY-ROAD (800-429-7623)
Co-branded Website: http://www.511vt.org

OPENING GREETING
"Welcome to 511 travel information brought to you by the Vermont Agency of Transportation. You can interrupt this message at any time if you know the route number that you want. For help with this system press pound – pound '##' or say 'help' at any time. Main Menu for road reports press or say one '1,' for regional reports press or say two '2,' for ferries and transit press or say three '3,' for tourism press or say four '4,' for nearby States' 511 press or say five '5,' for a live operator press or say six '6,' to comment on the 511 system press or say seven '7,' for help with the 511 system press pound – pound '##' or say 'help.'

911 Citation: No

BASIC MENU
1. Road Reports
2. Regional Reports
3. Ferries and Transit
4. Tourism
5. Nearby States 511
6. Live Operator
7. Comment on 511 System
\# Help With 511 System

TRANSIT MENU
For bus information in the State of Vermont you can visit www.vpta.net or you can call 1-800-685-7433 for bus routes, schedule, and ride share information.

WEATHER INFORMATION
Yes—Vermont Website takes you to the screen Vermont Travel Information Service. This screen provides two choices: low or high bandwidths. Click on low bandwidth to access screen which provides five locations within the State. The next screen provides a map and seven tabs with the fifth tab marked *Weather*. Click this tab to get seven day forecast for cities listed.

Connection/Referral to Transit Systems? Yes
Ability to Navigate up the Menu? Yes

Transfer to other 511 systems? Yes
Transfer to what other systems? New Hampshire, Rhode Island, Maine, Massachusetts, Quebec

Virginia 511

Date: March 2009

Phone Number: 800-578-4111
Co-branded Website: www.511virginia.org

OPENING GREETING
"Welcome to 511 Virginia, sponsored by the Virginia Department of Transportation—the options have changed. Main Menu: Please say the name of the interstate, bridge, tunnel or metro area for which you would like traffic information. To request traffic information for a city, county, or other roadway please say "traffic." You can also say "bridges and tunnels, public transportation, weather or more choices." Say 'feedback' to tell us what you think. Say 'main menu' to return to this menu. To return to the main menu press '9.' You may interrupt any menu with your choice at anytime.

911 Citation: No

BASIC MENU
1. Traffic
2. Public Transportation
3. Weather
4. More choices
    a. Other States
    b. Planned Construction
    c. Rest Areas
+ "Say 'feedback' to tell us what you think."

TRANSIT MENU
"Which city, county, commuter service or transit agency do you want to hear about? "

1. **Northern Virginia-Washington, D.C. Metro Area**
    a. Fairfax Connector Customer Service Office 703-339-7200
    b. Commuter Connections Systems Customer Service 800-745-7433
    c. Fairfax CUE Customer Service 703-385.7859 "I can transfer you. Do you want transferred?"
    d. WMATA. "I can transfer you to the Washington Metropolitan Area Transit Authority's (WMATA) Customer Service Department at 202-637-7000. Do you want transferred?"
    e. Alexandria DASH Customer Service 703-370-3274
    f. Arlington Regional Transit - ART Customer Service 703-228-7433
    g. Virginia Railway Express Customer Service 703-684-1001
    h. Loudoun County Customer Service 703-771-5665
    i. Purcellville Connector System Customer Service 877-777-2708
    j. Fairfax County RideSources Customer Service 703-324-1111
    k. PRTC OmniRide & Omnilink System Customer Service 703-730-6664

Virginia 511 ... continued

    l. Alexandria Rideshare Customer Service 703-838-3800
    m. George Transit Customer Service 202-637-7000 "I can transfer you. Do you want transferred?"

2. **Valley Metro.** (Valley Metro offers bus service for the Greater Roanoke Area.) I can transfer you to the Valley Metro Transit System at 540-982-2222. Do you want to be transferred?"

3. **Smart Way Bus System.** "I can transfer you to the Smart Way Bus System at 800-388-7075. Do you want to be transferred?"

4. **Richmond.** "I can transfer you to the GRTC transit system at 804-358-4782. Do you want to be transferred?

5. **Blacksburg/Christiansburg Transit.** (Blacksburg transit offers bus service for Virginia Tech and the Town of Blacksburg).
    a. "I can transfer you to the Blacksburg Transit System at 540-961-1185. Do you want to be transferred?"
    b. "I can transfer you to Smart Way Bus System at 800-388-7005. Do you want to be transferred?"
    c. "I can transfer you to Ride Solutions 540-342-9393."

6. **Harrisonburg Transit.** (Harrisonburg Transit offers bus service for the City of Harrisonburg and for James Madison University). I can transfer you to the Harrisonburg City Transit System at 540-432-0492. Do you want to be transferred?"

7. **Winchester Transit.** (Winchester Transit offers two public transportation services to the City of Winchester—a fixed route service and a paratransit service.) I can transfer you to the Winchester Transit System at 540-667-1815. Do you want to be transferred?"

WEATHER INFORMATION
YES—Virginia Website provides nine tabs; the eighth tab is Weather. Click on Weather and type in a zipcode for a 5-Day Weather Forecast for that location.

Connection/Referral to Transit Systems? Yes
Ability to Navigate up the Menu? Yes, "Press nine '9' or say 'main menu' at anytime."

Transfer to other 511 systems? Yes
Transfer to what other systems? North Carolina, Kentucky, Tennessee

Washington State

Date: March 2009

Phone Number: 800-695-7623
Co-branded Website: www.wsdot.wa.gov/traffic/511

OPENING GREETING
"This is the Washington State Department of Transportations 511 travel information system. If you prefer to speak your responses please remain on the line, or if you prefer to use our touch tone system, press pound '#' now. For Washington State ferry information say "ferry;" for mountain pass conditions say "mountain pass;" for current traffic conditions say "traffic;" for other travel information say "more choices;" for help at any time say 'help." This call could be monitored for quality assurance. Under 'more choices:' you can request; weather information, public transit telephone numbers, passenger rail telephone numbers, airline telephone numbers, travel information telephone numbers for adjacent States, provinces and cities, or express lane status. For help at any time `"' or press star '*'. To return to the main menu say "main menu" or press zero '0'."

911 Citation: No

BASIC MENU - *[Touch tone only]*

1. For Washington State Ferry information, press one '1'
2. For Current Traffic Conditions, press two '2'.
3. For Mountain Pass Conditions, press three '3'
4. To access the Oregon 511 system, press four '4'
5. For Express Lane Status, press five "5"
8. To repeat, press eight '8'

More Choices: [*Voice Recognition only*]
    a. Weather Information
    b. Public Transit Telephone Numbers
    c. Passenger Rail Telephone Numbers
    d. Airline Telephone Numbers
    e. Travel Information Telephone Numbers for adjacent States, provinces, and cities
    f. Express Lane Status

Washington State 511 ... continued

TRANSIT MENU
Note: Only through Voice Recognition and saying "more choices" - not through touch tone. You also need to know the name of the city or county.

1. **Seattle**
   a. Community Transit can be reached toll free at 800-562-1375 and locally at 425-348-7100.
   b. King County Metro can be reached at 206-553-3000.
   c. Sound Transit can be reached toll free at 888-889-6368.

2. **WalaWala** is served by Valley Transit. The telephone number is 509-525-9140

3. **Vancouver** is served by C-Tran. The telephone number is 360-696-4494.

4. **Olympia** is served by Intercity Transit. The telephone numbers are toll free at 800-287-6348 or locally at 360-786-8585

5. **Spokane Transit Authority** telephone number is 509-325-6000.

WEATHER INFORMATION
Yes—Washington State Website contains five tabs; first is entitled 'Traffic & Roads.' Click this tab which leads to Weather tab. This will provide real time weather information, seven-day forecasts, travel alerts, and slow downs.

Connection/Referral to Transit Systems? Yes
Ability to Navigate up the Menu? Yes

Transfer to other 511 systems? Yes
Transfer to what other systems? Oregon, Idaho (800-32-7623), British Columbia (900-565-4977)

Wisconsin

Date: April 2009

Phone Number: 866-511-WISC (9472)
Co-branded Website: www.511wi.gov

OPENING GREETING
"You've reached the Wisconsin 511 traveler information system brought to you by the Wisconsin Department of Transportation. Please be patient of the new 511 service is fine tuned. Please minimize background noise and speak clearly or you may switch to touch tone only mode by pressing star eight '*8' at any time. Do you want information about traffic and roads, public transit, roadside services, other services, or other States."

911 Citation: No

BASIC MENU
1. Traffic and Roads
2. Public Transit
3. Roadside Services
4. Other Services
    - Airports
    - Ride Share/Park and Rid
    - Department of Motor Vehicles
    - Wisconsin State Patrol
    - County Sheriff
5. Other States

TRANSIT MENU
1. Bus (name city for information)
2. Trains: a. Amtrak   b. Metra
3. Shared Taxis (name city for information)
4. Ferries
    a. Cassville Car Ferry   b. Lake Express
    c. Lake Michigan Car Ferry   d. Madeline Island Ferry Line
    e. Merrimac Ferry   f. Washington Island Ferry Line

WEATHER INFORMATION
Yes—Wisconsin Website contains five tabs of which the fourth is Travel Services. Select this tab for travel services screen which provides eight options of which the fourth option is weather. This option provides two choices: National Weather Service and Current Weather Conditions

Connection/Referral to Transit Systems? Yes
Ability to Navigate up the Menu? Yes
Transfer to other 511 systems? Yes
Transfer to what other systems? Iowa, Minnesota

Wyoming 511

Date: March 2009

Phone Number: 888-996-7623
Co-branded Website: www.wyoroad.info

OPENING GREETING
"Welcome to Wyoming's 511 travel information also on the web at [www.wyoroad.info]. This system uses voice recognition, to enable, press star '*' key now. For highway conditions press one '1', for tourism information press five '5', for information in other States press seven '7'."

911 Citation: No

BASIC MENU
1. Highway Conditions
5. Tourism Information
7. Information in Other States
    a. Colorado press one '1' (Call 1-303-639-1111)
    b. Nebraska press two '2'
    c. Utah press three '3' (Call 1-866-511-8824)
    d. South Dakota press four '4'
    e. Montana press five '5'
        1 Route specific information press one '1'
        2. Regional summary information press two '2'
    f. Idaho press six '6' (Call 1-888-432-7623)

TRANSIT MENU
No

WEATHER –
Yes—Wyoming Website [http://www.wyoroad.info/] contains eight options of which the fourth (new) option is entitled Conditions Maps. This option provides three choices:
- Observed Radar
- Observed Temperatures
- Observed Weather (updated every three hours)

Connection/Referral to Transit Systems? No
Ability to Navigate up the Menu? No

Transfer to other 511 systems? No
Transfer to what other systems? N.A.

B. METROPOLITAN 511 SYSTEMS WITH TRANSIT CONTENT

Cincinnati/Northern Kentucky

Date: February 2009

Phone Number: 513-333-3333
Co-branded Website: www.artimis.org

OPENING GREETING
"Welcome to the ARTIMIS [Advanced Regional Traffic Interactive Management & Information System] traveler information service. For express keypad entry pleas press the star '*' key now. For voice recognition and touch tone entry remain on the line. Please select one of the following menu items: for local traffic conditions press or say one '1', for statewide conditions press or say two '2', for transit information press or say three '3', for event information press or say four '4', for weather information press or say five '5', to provide feedback on this service press or say six '6', for tips on using the system press or say zero '0' for many of the menus."

911 Citation? No

BASIC MENU
1. Local Traffic Conditions
2. Statewide Conditions
3. Transit Information
4. Event Information
5. Weather Information
6. Feedback on this Service
7. Tips on Using the System

TRANSIT MENU
"The following transit information is available:
1. **For Cincinnati** bus travel information and transportation to and from special events, press or say one '1'.
2. **For Northern Kentucky** bus information and travel to and from special events, press or say two '2'.
3. **For additional information for Metro**, TANK [Transit Authority of Northern Kentucky], ride share and alternative transportation, press or say three '3'.

Cincinnati/Northern Kentucky ...continued

"Welcome to the ARTIMIS alternative transportation information Hotline, please listen to the following options available:
    a To be transferred to Cincinnati Metro bus service, press or say one '1'.
    b To be transferred to TANK bus service, press or say two '2'.
    c To be transferred to rideshare, press or say three '3'.
    d To be transferred to airport shuttle and limousine service, press or say four '4'.
    e To be transferred to Butler County RTA, press or say five '5'.
    f To be transferred to Warren County Transit Service, press or say six '6'.
    g To be transferred to Claremont County Transportation Connection, press or say seven '7'.
    h To return to the main menu, press or say nine '9'".

WEATHER INFORMATION
No—Cincinnati/Northern Kentucky Website [http://www.artimis.org/]does not contain weather related information.

Connection/Referral to Transit Systems? Yes
Ability to navigate up the Menu? Yes

Transfer to other 511 systems? No
Transfer to what other systems? N.A.

Jacksonville/Northeast Florida

Date: March 2009

Phone Number: 866-511-3352
Co-branded Website: www.JAX511.com

OPENING GREETING
"You've reached the Northeast Florida travel information service brought to you by the Florida Department of Transportation Say "main menu" to return to this menu. Press '88' or 'tt.' at anytime to switch to touch tone mode. Now do you want information about highways, public transit, airports, sports complex, other parts of the State or press the pound '#' key to tell us what you think."

911 Citation? No

BASIC MENU
1. Highways
2. Public Transit
3. Airports
4. Sports Complex
5. Other 511 Systems Within the State
\# Tell us what you think.

TRANSIT MENU
Jacksonville Transit Authority

WEATHER INFORMATION
NO—Jacksonville/Northeast Florida Website does not provide weather information unless it is hurricane related.

Connection/Referral to Transit Systems? Yes

Ability to navigate up the Menu? Yes

Transfer to other 511 systems? Yes
Transfer to what other systems? Florida Statewide, Southeast Florida, Southwest Florida, Central Florida, Tampa Bay

Missouri – St. Louis Gateway 511

Date: March 2009

Phone Number: 877-478-5511
Co-branded Website: [http://www.modot.org/stlouis/index.htm]

OPENING GREETING
"Traffic.com. Hello and welcome to Gateway Guide 511 Traveler Information Service brought to you by Missouri (MO) DOT. For other transportation options please say 'directory' at any time. What road do you want?"

911 Citation? No

BASIC MENU
[Note: "Say 'directory' to hear the following: "Here are a few important numbers to help you get around St. Louis.]

1. To reach MO DOT, call 1-888-275-6636
2. For Missouri Highway Patrol, phone 1-800-525-5555
3. Illinois DOT is at 1-217-782-7820
4. St. Louis Metro Information is at 1-314-231-2345
5. Missouri Road Conditions is at 1-800-222-6400

"Just say 'Directory' at any time to hear this list again. What road do you want?"

TRANSIT MENU
St. Louis Metro Information: 1-314-231-2345.

WEATHER INFORMATION
No—St.Louis Gateway does not contain weather information [http://www.traffic.com/St-Louis-Traffic/St-Louis-Traffic-roads.ht]

Connection/Referral to Transit Systems? Yes
Ability to Navigate up the Menu? Yes.

Transfer to other 511 systems? No.
Transfer to what other systems? N.A.

Orlando/Central Florida

Date: March 2009

Phone Number: 866-510-1930
Co-branded Website: www.fl511.com

OPENING GREETING
"Welcome to Central Florida's travel information system. Say "highways" or press one '1,' say "public transportation" or press two '2,' say "airports" or press three '3,' say "Port Canaveral" or press four '4,' say "other parts of the State" or press five '5,' or you can say "feedback" or press the pound key '#' to tell us what you think."

911 Citation? No

BASIC MENU
[Note: To switch to touch-tone mode, press '88']

1. Highway Conditions
2. Public Transportation
3. Airports
4. Port Canaveral
5. Other Parts of the State
\# Feedback

TRANSIT MENU
"I can transfer you to transit information, Access LYNX or carpools. Say "transit information" or press one '1.' Say "Access LYNX" or press two '2'. Say "carpool" or press three '3'."

1. **Transit Information**.
   You have reached LYNX customer service. For fixed route bus assistance press one '1'; for lost and found press two '2'; for customer relations, concerns, compliments, and suggestions press three '3'; for information concerning advertising press four '4'; for Access LYNX press five '5'; for LYNX jobline press eight '8'; for carpools and van pools transportation assistance press nine '9'; to repeat this message press seven '7'."
   1. Fixed Route Bus Assistance
   2. Lost and Found
   3. Customer Relations
   4. Information Concerning Advertising
   5. Access LYNX

Orlando/Central Florida  ... continued

6. Repeat Message
7. LYNX Job Line
8. Carpools and Van Pools Transportation Assistance

2. **ACCESS LYNX**
   a. "To check on the arrival of your vehicle for today, select option three '3'.
   b. If you would like to make a reservation for tomorrow or up to seven days in advance, cancel trips more than one day in advance or multiple trip changes, select option four '4'.
   c. To make comments or suggestions about Access LYNX, select option five '5'.
   d. Questions concerning eligibility, select option six '6'.
   e. To cancel your reservation for today with less than 24 hours notice, select option seven '7'"..
   f. To schedule a pick up, select option eight '8'

3. **Carpool**
   "You have reached the LYNX Ride Share Line for Carpooling, Vanpooling to work and Adopt a Stop program,. If you are calling to make door-to-door pickup for persons with special needs, please contact Access LYNX Department at 407-423-8747. Otherwise, Please leave your name, number and a brief message and we will get back to you." *Note*: An employee responds to inquiries from 8:00 am to 5:00 pm Monday through Friday.

WEATHER INFORMATION
No.

Connection/Referral to Transit Systems? Yes
Ability to Navigate up the Menu? Yes

Transfer to other 511 systems? Yes
Transfer to what other systems? Northeast Florida, Southeast Florida, Southwest Florida, Tampa Bay, or Statewide Florida

Sacramento/Northern California 511

Date: March 2009

Phone Number: 877-511-TRIP [8747]
Co-branded Website: www.sacregion511.org

OPENING GREETING
"Welcome to 511 your travel guide to the Sacramento Region and Northern California. For English press one '1' [Spanish Insert]. For information on downtown Sacramento I-5 construction project press five '5'; For Sacramento, Yolo, Placer, El Dorado, Yuba and Sutter Counties press one '1'; for Bay Area 511 System press two '2'; for all other northern California areas including the Tahoe Basin press three '3'; for the National Weather Service, other 511 systems or 50Corridor.com information press four '4'."

911 Citation: No

BASIC MENU
1. Sacramento, Yolo, Placer, El Dorado, Yuba and Sutter Counties
    a. Highway Information, press one '1'
    b. Transit Information Including Public Transit Service to the Sacramento International Airport, press two '2'
    c. Car Pooling, Van Pooling, Bicycling or Telecommuting, press three '3'
    d. Amtrak Information, press four '4'
2. Bay Area 511 System, press two '2' [Note: Press zero '0' for the touch tone menu listed below.]
    1. Traffic menu, press one '1'
    2. Public Transportation menu. press two '2'
    3. Freeway Aid, press three '3'
    4. Translink, press four '4'
    5. My 511, press five '5'
    6. Transit Departure Times, press six '6'
    7. Ridesharing, press seven '7'
    8. Bicycling, press eight '8'
    9. Fast-Trax, press nine '9'
    10. Sacramento 511, press ten '10' '
    11. Traffic conditions, press eleven '11'
    12. Driving Times, press twelve '12'
    13. Airports, press thirteen '13'
    14. Paratransit, press fourteen '14'
    15. Transit Agencies, press fifteen '15'
    16. AC Transit, pres sixteen '16'

Sacramento/Northern California 511 ...Continued

       17. Muni, press seventeen '17'
       18. BART, press eighteen '18'
       19. BTA, press nineteen '19'
       20. Cal-train, press twenty '20'
       21. Golden Gate Transit, press twenty-one '21'
       22. San-Tran, press twenty-two '22'
       23. All-Nighter, press twenty-three '23'

3. All Other Northern California Areas Including the Tahoe Basin
    a. Highway Information, press one '1'
    b. Transit Information for the Tahoe-Truckee Area, Nevada, Butte, and Glenn Counties, press two '2'
    c. Carpooling, Vanpooling, Bicycling, or Telecommuting, press three '3'
    d. Amtrak Information, press four '4'

4. National Weather Service, Other 511 Systems, for 50Corridor.com Information
    a. National Weather Service, press one '1'
    b. Nevada 511 System, press two '2'
    c. Oregon 511 System, press three '3'
    d. 50Corridor.com Information, press four '4'

TRANSIT MENU

1. **"For Sacramento County transit** information including public transit service to the Sacramento International Airport, press one '1'"
    a. Regional Transit Bus and Light Rail Information, press one '1'
    b. Public transit service to the Sacramento International Airport, press two '2'
    c. Paratransit Service, press three '3'
    d. Folsom Stage Line, press four '4'
    e. CSUS [California State University-Sacramento] Shuttle, press five '5'
    f. South County Transit, press six '6'
    g. E-tran in Elk Grove, press seven '7'

2. **"For Yolo County transit** information including public transit service to the Sacramento International Airport, press two '2'"
    a. Yolobus including public transit service to the Sacramento International Airport, press one '1'
    b. Unitrans [University Transport System] Bus Service, press two '2'
    c. Davis Community Transit curb to curb transportation service with priority to qualified elderly and disabled persons, press three '3'

Sacramento/Northern California 511 ...continued

3. **"For Placer and El Dorado Counties** transit information, press three '3'"
   A. **Placer County Transit press one '1'**
      1. CTSA [Consolidated Transportation Services Agency] for elderly and disabled persons including Auburn, Granite Bay, Rockland and Lewis Dial-a-Ride press two '2'
      2. City of Roseville Transit including commuter service press three '3'
      3. City of Auburn Transit press four '4'
      4. City of Lincoln Transit press five '5'
      5. North Lake Tahoe-Truckee Transit press six '6'
      6. Addition questions concerning transit services in Placer County press seven '7'
   B. **El Dorado County Transit Services** including commuter services, press two '2'

4. **"For Yuba and Sutter Counties transit** information including Sacramento commuter service, press four '4'
5. **"For Tahoe-Truckee Area and Nevada County** press one '1'"
   a. North Lake Tahoe-Truckee Transit, press one '1'
   b. Gold Country Stage serving Western Nevada County and Auburn, press two '2'
   c. Blue-Go Transit serving South Lake Tahoe, press three '3'
6. **"For Butte and Glenn Counties** press two '2'"
   A. Butte County Transit press one '1'
      a. Chico Area Transit, press one '1'
      b. Oroville Area Transit, press one '1'
      c. Paradise Express, press one '1'
   B. Glenn County Transit including Glenn Ride with service to Chico, press two '2'

WEATHER INFORMATION
Yes—Sacramento/Northern California Website provides three options. Click on the first option entitled Traffic. This contains seven choices of which the sixth is *Weather*. The Weather screen has a number of weather related topics from which to choose:
- *Current Hazards*--Watches/Warnings, Local Outlook, National Outlooks;
- *Current Conditions*--Observations, Radar Imagery, Satellite Imagery, Soundings/Profilers, Rivers & Lakes, AHPS, River Levels, Precipitation, Buoy Reports, Road Conditions;
- *Forecasts*--Activity Planner, Local Forecasts, AFD-Discussion, Prototype Digital, Forecasts, Aviation, Fire Weather, Hydrology, Marine, Computer Models;
- *Climate*—Local, National;
- *Weather Safety*—Weather Radio, Safety Tips, Storm Ready.

Connection/Referral to Transit Systems: Yes
Ability to Navigate up the Menu: Yes
Transfer to other 511 systems: Yes
Transfer to what other systems: Nevada, Oregon

San Diego

Date: March 2009

Phone Number: 800-215-4551
Co-branded Website: www.511sd.com/

OPENING GREETING
"Welcome to 511 San Diego County's traffic, transit, and commuter information service. Also visit us on the web at: www.511sd.com. Main menu: [Note: Press one '1' if you want the instructions in Spanish]. I can give you information on: traffic, public transportation, roadside assistance, ridesharing, taxis and shuttles, or more choices. Which one would you like? Say 'what are my choices" for a list of everything you can do or say "help." Now what can I get you? You can also go directly to any of the following-- [airports, Fastrak, bicycling, guaranteed ride home, arrive alive, school pool, traffic conditions, driving times, border crossing, or compass card.] To hear these again say "repeat". Which would you like? "
911 Citation: No

BASIC MENU
1. Traffic
2. Public Transportation
3. Road Side Assistance
4. Ride Sharing
5. Taxis & Shuttles
6. More Choices
   - Airports
   - Fastrak
   - Bicycling
   - Guaranteed Ride Home
   - Arrive Alive
   - School Pool
   - Traffic Conditions
   - Driving Times
   - Border Crossing
   - Compass Card

TRANSIT MENU
1. Buses
   a. Lost and Found
   b. Info Express for Bus Schedule
   c. Transit Information Specialist
   d. Departure Times
   e. Operator

San Diego 511 ...continued

TRANSIT MENU...continued

2. Trolleys
   a. Lost and Found
   b. Operator

3. The Coaster
   a. Lost and Found
   b. Special Events
   c. Operator

4. Paratransit
   Caller must name the paratransit agency or city.

5. Commuter Train - Transfers caller to:
   a. AMTRAK
   b. Metro-Link
   c. The Coaster
   d. Information on the Sprinter Train

WEATHER INFORMATION
No—Weather information is not provided by Website or 511 telephone call.

Connection/Referral to Transit Systems? Yes
Ability to Navigate up the Menu? Yes

Transfer to other 511 systems? No
Transfer to what other systems? N.A.

San Francisco

Date: March 2009

Phone Number: 866-736-7433
Co-branded Website: http://www.511.org

OPENING GREETING
"Welcome to the Bay Area's 511. Main menu: I can give you information on: traffic, public transportation, freeway aid, translink, or more choices. Say which you'd like? Or press zero '0' for touch tone. To hear a complete list of what is available say "what are my choices?" You can also interrupt me or say "help" at anytime. Now what can I get you?"

911 Citation: No

BASIC MENU
(To start over at any time just say "main menu")

1. Traffic Menu, press one '1'
2. Public Transportation, press two '2'
3. Freeway Aid, press three '3'
4. TransLink, press four '4'
5. My 511, press five '5'
6. Transit Departure Times, press six '6'
7. Ride Sharing, press seven '7'
8. Bicycling, press eight '8'
9. FasTrak, press nine '9'
10. Sacramento 511, press ten '10'

11. Traffic Conditions, press eleven '11'
12. Driving Times, press twelve '12'
13. Airports, press thirteen '13'
14. Paratransit, press fourteen '14'
15. Transit Agencies, press fifteen '15'
16. AC Transit, press sixteen '16'
17. MUNI, press seventeen '17'
18. BART, press eighteen '18'
19. VTA, press nineteen '19'
20. Cal-train press twenty '20'
21. Golden Gate Transit, press twenty-one '21'
22. Santran press twenty-two '22'
23. All-nighter Service, press twenty-three '23'

San Francisco 511 ... continued

TRANSIT MENU

1. **Transit Agencies** - You need to know the name of the transit agency or provide the name of the city you are traveling from.

    a. AC Transit
    b. Caltrain Central Contra Costa TA
    c. Valley Transportation Authority
    d. Santrans [San Francisco Muni]
    e. San Mateo County TD
    f. Tri-Delta Transit
    g. Vallejo Transit
    h. Golden Gate Transit [GGT]
        1. Ferry 2. Bus
    i. BGF [Blue and Gold Ferry]
    j. AITFC [Angel Island-Tiburon Ferry Company]
    k. San Francisco BART [Bay Area Rapid Transit]
    l. San Mateo CityBus
    m. Modesto MAX [Modesto Area Express]
    n. San Joaquin RTD [Regional Transportation]
    o. HBF [Harbor Bay Ferry]
    p. Capitol Corridor
    q. VBF [Vallejo Baylink Ferry]
    r. WestCAT [Western Contra Costa Transit Authority]
    s. Wheels [Livermore/Amador Valley Transit Authority, LAVTA]
    t. UCT [Union City Transit]
    u. EGR [Emery GoRound]
    v. AOFS [Alameda/Oakland Ferry Service]
    w. ACE [Altamont Commuter Express]

2. **Departure Times** now available for BART

3. **Trans Links** - Transfers you to the translink customer service center.

4. **Commuter Incentives** - Programs that provide commuters with monetary rewards as alternatives to traveling alone.

San Francisco 511 ... continued

5. **Airports**
    a. San Francisco International
    b. Oakland International
    c. San Jose
    d. Sacramento

6. **Paratransit** - You need to know the name of the county or provide the name of the city you are traveling from.
    a. SFP [San Francisco Paratransit]
    b. EBPC [East Bay Paratransit Consortium]
    c. Wheels Dial-a-Ride [City of Pleasanton Paratransit Service]
    d. Union City Para transit

7. **All-nighter Service** - Transfers you to all-nighter service operator.

WEATHER INFORMATION
No – San Francisco Bay Area Website does not provide weather information.

Connection/Referral to Transit Systems? Yes
Ability to Navigate up the Menu? Yes

Transfer to other 511 systems? Yes
Transfer to what other systems? Sacramento

Southeast Florida

Date: March 2009

Phone Number: 866-914-3838
Co-branded Website: http://www.southflorida511.com

OPENING GREETING
"You've reached the Sun Guide traffic and public transit travel information service for South Florida--brought to you by the Florida Department of Transportation and the Miami-Dade Expressway Authority. [Para Espanol---Spanish text insert]. Please note that our system has changed. If you already know your route code, enter it followed by the pound '#' or number sign key instead of the star '*' key. Now you can choose to hear information about: highways, public transit, other services or other 511 systems. Which would you like? "

911 Citation: No

BASIC MENU
[Note: Press eight-eight '88' to switch to touch tone only mode]

"Press one '1' for highways; press two '2' for public transit; press three '3' for other services; press four '4' for other 511 systems. To give feedback press the pound '#' key and press the star '*' key .to hear your options again."
1. Highways
2. Public Transit
3. Other Services
4. Other 511 Systems
'#*' Feedback

TRANSIT MENU
"Welcome to the Sun Guide public transit travel information service line. If you need instructions say 'help'. You can press eight-eight '88' or 'tt' for touch tone. Press one '1' for Broward County Transit, press two '2' for Miami-Dade, press three '3' for Palm Tran, press four '4' for Tri-Rail or press five '5' for South Florida's Ride Sharing and Emergency Ride Services. Press the star '*' key to hear your options again."

1. Broward County Transit
   a. Schedule, press '1'
   b. Fares, press '2'
   c. General Information, press '3'
      1. For the Lost and Found Department, press '1'
      2. For Special Events, press '2'
      3. To talk to an agent who can assist you with trip planning, press '3'
      4. To make a comment, complaint or suggestion, press '4'

Southeast Florida 511 ... continued

     5. For More Options, press '5'
         a. To learn about taking your bicycle on the bus or wheelchair accessibility, press '1'
         b. For maps and schedules by mail, press '2'
         c. Or to learn about TOPS [Transportation Options] for those with disabilities that prevent them from using regular fixed route bus transportation, press '3'
     6. Or to select another transit system, press '6' now
- d. To choose another transit authority, press '4'
- e. To return to this menu, press '9' at any time

2. Miami-Dade Transit
  a. Schedule, press '1'
  b. Fares, press '2'
  c. General Information, press '3'
      1. For the Lost and Found Department, press '1'
      2. For Special Events, press '2'
      3. To talk to an agent who can assist you with trip planning, press '3'
      4. To make a comment, complaint or suggestion, press '4'
      5. For More Options, press '5'
          - To learn about taking your bicycle on transit, press '1'
          - To hear about wheelchair accessibility, press '2'
          - For maps and schedules by mail, press '3'
          - Or to learn about special transportation services for those who can not use regular public transportation, press '4'
      6. Or to select another transit system, press '6' now

  d. To choose another transit authority, press '4'
  e. To return to this menu, press '9' at any time

3. Palm Tran
  a. Schedule, press '1'
  b. Fares, press '2'
  c. General Information, press '3
      1. For the Lost and Found Department, press '1'
      2. For Special Events, press '2'
      3. To talk to an agent who can assist you with trip planning, press '3'
      4. To make a comment, complaint or suggestion, press '4'
      5. For More Options, press '5'
          - To learn about taking your bicycle on the bus and wheelchair accessibility, press '1'

Southeast Florida 511 ... continued

- For maps and schedules by mail, press '2'
- Or to learn about special transportation services for those who can not use regular public transportation, press '3'
6. Or to select another transit system, press '6' now

d. To Choose another Transit Authority, press '4'
e. To return to this menu, press '9' at any time

4: Tri- Rail
a. Schedule, press '1'
b. Fares, press '2'
c. General Information, press '3'
 1. For the Lost and Found Department, press '1'
 2. For Special Events, press '2'
 3. To talk to an agent who can assist you with trip planning, press '3'
 4. To make a comment, complaint or suggestion, press '4'
 5. For More Options, press '5'
    - To learn about taking your bicycle on the train or wheelchair accessibility, press '1'
    - For maps and schedules by mail, press '2'
    - Or to select another transit system, press '6' now
d To Choose Another Transit Authority, press '4'
e. To return to this menu, press '9' at any time

5: South Florida's Ridesharing and Emergency Ride Services
"Commuters who use transit at least three times a week are eligible for the emergency ride home program. It will provide free taxi service in emergency situations for registered commuters in Broward, Miami-Dade, and Palm Beach Counties twenty-four hours a day, seven days a week. I can transfer you to the customer service center at 1-800-234-RIDE [7433] twenty-four hours a day. Would you like to be transferred? Press '1' for yes or '2' for no."

WEATHER INFORMATION
Southeast Florida Website contains six tabs. Weather alerts provided when needed.

Connection/Referral to Transit Systems? Yes
Ability to Navigate up the Menu? Yes

Transfer to other 511 systems? Yes
Transfer to what other systems? Central Florida, 511 Tampa Bay, Florida Statewide

Southwest Florida

Date: March 2009

Phone Number: 866-511-3352
Co-branded Website: www.southwestflorida511.com

OPENING GREETING

"You have reached the Southwest Florida travel information service brought to you by the Florida Department of Transportation. Say "main menu" to return to this menu. Press '88' or 'tt.' at any time to switch to touch tone mode. For highways press one '1', for public transit press two '2', for the airport press three '3', for other 511systems press four '4', to give feedback press the pound '#" key. Press the star '*' key to hear your options again."

911 Citation? No

BASIC MENU
1. Highways
2. Public Transit
3. Airport
4. Other 511 Systems
\# Tell us what you think
* To hear options again

TRANSIT MENU   [Automatic transfer]
1. For Lee Tran (Lee County Transit) press one '1'
2. For Charlotte Transit press two '2'
3. For Collier Area Transit (CAT) press three '3'

WEATHER INFORMATION
Yes - Website provides weather forecast when needed for Port Charlotte, FT. Myers, and Naples Metro areas.

Connection/Referral to Transit Systems? Yes
Ability to navigate up the Menu? Yes

Transfer to other 511 systems? Yes
Transfer to what other systems? Central Florida, Florida Statewide, Northeast Florida, Southeast Florida, 511 Tampa Bay

Tampa Bay

Date: April 2009

Phone Number: 800-576-3886
Co-branded Website: www.511tampabay.com

OPENING GREETING
"Welcome to 511 Tampa Bay. Do you want traffic or other services? If you are new to 511 Tampa Bay, try saying 'help' now." Do you want traffic information on select Tampa area roads or other services? If you are new to 511 Tampa Bay, try saying 'help' now." If you select other service, do you want transit or events information? To reach a different 511 system say "transfer." To record a comment say 'record a comment.' Say "help" anytime for assistance with the main menu. Say 'main menu' to get back to main menu at anytime. It's ok to interrupt me if you want to ask me something.'
911 Citation: No

BASIC MENU
1. Traffic conditions
2. Transit
3. Events
4. Other 511 System

TRANSIT MENU.
You need to know the name of the mass transit system, airport, or seaport.
Note: For non-residents, to identify transit agencies, say "list."
1. Bay Area Commuter Service [BACS] Connection number is 800-9-7433
2. Lakeland Area Mass Transit Citrus "Connection number is 863-688-7433"
3. HART [Hillsborough Area Regional Transportation] "Info number is 813-254-4278 "
4. Manatee County Area Transit [MCAT] "MCAT number is 941-747-8621 ext 227"
5. Pasco County Public Transportation [PCPT] "Information number is 727-834-3322"
6. St Petersburg-Clearwater International Airport "General Info number is 727-453-7800"
7. Port of Tampa "Main Office number is 813-905-7678 or 800-741-2297"
8. Sarasota Bradenton Airport "General Information number is 941-359-2770"
9. PSTA [Pinellas Suncoast Transit Authority] "Info line number is 727-530-9911"
10. Tampa International Airport "General Information number is 813-870-8770"
11. Tampa Union Station "Service number is 800-USA-RAIL [800-872-7245]"

WEATHER INFORMATION- *No,* Tampa Bay Website does not provide weather information.

Connection/Referral to Transit Systems? Yes, if you know the name of the system you will be given contact information.
Ability to Navigate up the Menu? Yes, just say "main menu" at any time.
Transfer to other 511 systems? Yes
Transfer to what other systems? Statewide System, Orlando System, Miami-Dade County

Forty-Three 511 Systems: Areas of Commonality and Uniqueness
April 2009

1. *All systems* have co-branded web sites.

2. *Thirty-eight systems* begin their 511 menus with highway/traffic information. [Georgia 511 menu begins with reports on incidents, accidents and motor assistance; New Jersey 511 menu starts with urban areas; New York 511 menu is provided by region; Washington State 511 begins its menu with transit 'ferry service' information]

3. *Thirty-three* are Statewide systems [Ten are Metro: Central Florida, Cincinnati/ Northern Kentucky, Northeast Florida, Sacramento/ Northern California, San Diego, San Francisco Bay Area, Southeast Florida, Southwest Florida, St. Louis Gateway, Tampa Bay]

4. *Thirty-one systems* provide weather information usually associated with road conditions affecting the interstate and State highways - [Alaska, California Eastern Sierra, Cincinnati/Northern Kentucky, Colorado, Georgia, Idaho, Iowa, Kansas, Kentucky Statewide, Louisiana, Maine, Minnesota, Montana, Nebraska, New Hampshire, New Jersey, New Mexico, Nevada, North Carolina, North Dakota, Rhode Island, Sacramento/Northern California, San Diego, South Dakota, Southwest Florida, Tennessee, Vermont, Virginia, Washington State, Wisconsin, and Wyoming]

5. *Twenty-four systems* provide public transit information [Arizona, Cincinnati/ Northern Kentucky, Central Florida, Georgia, Maine, Massachusetts, Minnesota, New Hampshire, New York, Northeast Florida, North Carolina, Rhode Island, Sacramento/Northern California, San Francisco Bay Area, San Diego, Southeast Florida, Southwest Florida, St. Louis Gateway, Tampa Bay, Utah, Vermont, Virginia, Washington State, Wisconsin]. *Sixteen systems* will automatically transfer, if requested, to a transit provider [Arizona, Cincinnati/Northern Kentucky, Georgia, Maine, Massachusetts, Minnesota, New York, North Carolina, Orlando/Central Florida, Sacramento/Northern California, San Diego, San Francisco Bay Area, Southeast Florida, Southwest Florida, Virginia, and Wisconsin]. The transit information is for bus, rail and ferry services and sometimes airport services as well. This transit information may also include Paratransit, Dial-a-Ride and route deviation services available to those local residents who are eligible for these services.

6. *Twenty-three systems* will transfer the caller to another 511 system [Central Florida, Florida Statewide, Georgia, Kentucky Statewide, Maine, Nevada, New Hampshire, New Mexico, New York, North Carolina, Oregon, Rhode Island, Sacramento/Northern California, San Francisco Bay Area, Southeast Florida, Southwest Florida, Tampa Bay, Tennessee, Utah, Vermont, Virginia, Washington State, and Wisconsin]

7. *Eighteen systems* provide an opportunity for the caller to give feedback on the 511 service [Alaska, Arizona, Cincinnati/ Northern Kentucky, Florida Statewide, Kentucky Statewide, Louisiana, Minnesota, New Hampshire, New Jersey, New York, North Carolina, Oregon, Rhode Island, Southeast Florida, Southwest Florida, Tennessee, Vermont, and Virginia]

8. *Eleven systems* provide the caller with information on tourism sites within the State [Arizona, Georgia, Idaho, Kentucky Statewide, Maine, Montana, New Hampshire, Rhode Island, Southwest Florida, Vermont, and Wyoming]

9. *Eleven systems* provide information on ferry or water transport services [Alaska, Maine, Massachusetts, New York, North Carolina, San Francisco Bay Area, Rhode Island, Utah, Vermont, Washington State, and Wisconsin]

10. *Seven systems* use a motto for their 511 systems: "Travel in the Know" [Alaska], "We're Here to Get You There" [California Eastern Sierra], "Keeps Central Florida Moving" [Central Florida], "We'll Get You There" [Georgia], "Get Connected To Go" [New York], "Keep Moving" [Northeast Florida],"Know Before You Go" Southwest Florida].

11. *Seven systems* caution callers to hang up and call 911 if in an emergency situation [Kansas, Massachusetts, Nebraska, New Mexico, North Dakota, Rhode Island and South Dakota]

12. *Two 511 systems* share a common website [Central Florida and Florida Statewide].

The Nation's  *Traveler Information Service*

**Office of Research, Demonstration and Innovation
U.S. Department of Transportation
1200 New Jersey Avenue, SE
Washington, DC 20590
http://www.fta.dot.gov/research**

Report No. FTA-TRI30-2009.1

www.ingramcontent.com/pod-product-compliance
Lightning Source LLC
Chambersburg PA
CBHW081843170526
45167CB00007B/2893